Sex in the Outdoors

a humorous approach to recreation

by Robert Rose, M.D. &
Buck Tilton

Illustrations by Marc Bohne

ICS BOOKS, Inc.
Merrillville, Indiana

SEX IN THE OUTDOORS: a humorous approach to recreation
Copyright © 1993 by Buck Tilton

10 9 8 7 6 5 4 3 2 1

Printed in U.S.A.

All ICS titles are printed on 50% recycled paper for pre-consumer waste. All sheets are processed without using acid.

Published by:
ICS Books, Inc.
1370 E. 86th Place
Merrillville, IN 46410
800-541-7323

Library of Congress Cataloging-in-Publication Data

Rose, Robert, 1948-
    Sex in the outdoors : a humorous approach to recreation / by Robert Rose & Buck Tilton.
        p.   cm.
      Includes index.
      ISBN 0-934802-86-6 : $6.99
      1. Sex instruction. 2. Outdoor recreation. I. Tilton, Buck.
    II. Title.
    HQ23.R67 1993
    306.7--dc20   93-27919
                                                          CIP

Ways to Enjoy Sex in the Outdoors

TABLE OF CONTENTS

Appendices

Introduction to the Preface

"When ideas fail, words come in very handy." Goethe.

If anybody takes anything in this book seriously, they could be in serious trouble because: 1) Life is far too short to be taken seriously. And 2) If anything in this book bears any resemblance to anything true, it is a serious mistake. These words are intended to be entertainment. If the reader gets any ideas, that's great! But don't try this stuff in your own backyard, kids . . . at least not without adult supervision.

Preface to the Introduction

"There are strange things done in the midnight sun . . ." Robert Service.

Anybody can have sex indoors. Well, almost anybody. This book is not about things like positions to do it in, pathways to do it with, or problems associated with doing it at all. Those things are the same no matter where you go . . . or come. This book is about doing it outdoors.

Sex in the Outdoors: Introduction

"Truth is erotic." Margo Anand.

Why write a book about sex in the outdoors? To tell the truth, when I confided to a few select friends and colleagues that I was working on this book (I was seeking interesting anecdotes, not bragging . . . at least that's what I told them), the most common response was: What in hell for? So I came up with this answer: If you are one of those people who are content to flounder along as you always have, possibly putting yourself and maybe other people in a risky situation, ignorant of your impact on a fragile ecosystem, oblivious to the possible variations that would make life much more interesting, unaware of the subtle context in which you are doing "it", and out of touch with higher philosophical thought that gives meaning to otherwise mere sensual behavior, then this book is not for you. But, if you are among the enlightened minority who prefer to enter the outdoor world prepared to protect yourself, sensitive to not even leaving footprints (or buttprints), desirous of enjoying a full variety of experiences and being in harmony with natural surroundings while your consciousness is raised to new heights, then this book is for you. This book may also be for you if you bought a bottle of wine but your date canceled out for this evening, there's nothing good on TV, and you're looking for something to read.

Why write a book about sex in the outdoors? The notice on my kitchen wall constantly reminds me: Good lovin' don't last, good cookin' do! But that isn't necessarily so. The point is this: There is a difference between a delicately seasoned and carefully prepared filet mignon and a hunk of beef blackened over an open fire. Good cooking, like good sex, doesn't happen naturally. First, one decides what one wants to eat. Then a few hints are listened to, a recipe is read, and, perhaps, you are shown, on your initial try, how to do it right. It's difficult to make a hollandaise sauce by trial and error. Although, admittedly, it might be more fun to cook up some outdoor sex through experimentation, there is a backpack full of reasons to have a guidebook. The main reason is this: Who enjoys burned steak?

Why write a book about sex in the outdoors? For some the question might arise from simple unfamiliarity with the wild. Most people have, at least, a passing knowledge of sex, but they go into the outdoors only occasionally, and have thought little of putting the two together. (Note: This is especially true of people whose outdoor experiences are limited to Scout outings and family excursions in single, big-walled tent.) For some the days of an outdoor trip are filled with making and breaking camp, moving from one place to another, preparing and eating meals, dealing with the weather and, generally, smushing as much non-sexual activity into the hours as possible. However, with a little planning, the smile of fickle fate, and determination, anyone can squeeze some sex into every outdoor adventure. You don't have to leave home without it.

Why write a book about sex in the outdoors? Somebody had to do it!

1

The History of
Sex in the Outdoors

"Those who are ignorant of history are doomed to make the same stupid mistakes again." My Mother, shortly after my first birthday.

Somewhere between four and five bazillion years ago, give or take a wild weekend or two, those ape-like creatures spoken of today as "pre-humans" began to chill out, in a most literal sense. That is to say they started getting cold because the whole earth was cooling off after a tumultuous and very hot beginning. Driven from a lush life well off the ground in the leafy trees that had always been home, they began to move south, where it was warmer, onto the vast grassy savannahs of what is now known as Africa. Shuffling along on hands and feet proved painfully slow, but all the other creatures of the savannah were doing it and pre-human brains were fairly small and not especially creative. Eventually, however, somebody starting walking upright, it caught on, and humans became bipeds. Becoming bipedal was, perhaps, the most critical moment in the development of sex-as-fun, as opposed to the old concept of sex-as-merely-reproduction-of-the-species.

Prior to bipedalism, people's physical views of each other were limited; a hunched over clump of matted hair and maybe a hairy butt-shot now and then. Sex was a once-a-year instinctual urge, just like the doggies were doing it, over in moments and less satisfying

1

than the discovery of a banana or a mango. At this time the only warm fuzzy feelings occurred during the sex act itself. But, suddenly, everyone's sexual organs were hanging out on display for all the world to see. Individualism began to take on a wholly unique meaning. This new view began to tingle a few primitive imaginations. Added to the visual impact of being bipedal was the fact that arms and hands, previously used most of the time for clinging to tree limbs, now had hours and hours of spare time to deal with. And there wasn't an awful lot to cling to on the African savannahs. Furthermore, it was cold, particularly at night, and temperature had a definite and substantial effect on the history of sex in the outdoors (see Environmental Exposure). One chilly night, long after the mating season had ended, a pre-human, probably a male (since males have less body fat and cool off quicker), suggested to another pre-human, probably a female (since the visible body parts were different and more interesting), that they have sex. She went for the idea, that caught on also, and, God bless their long-departed souls, it continues today.

Primitive Opening Line: "You want bite of my banana?"

Little is known about sex in the outdoors over the next few million years. One of the few truly relevant discoveries, which got almost no publicity, is credited to the Leakeys, who have recovered some of the oldest remains of primitive humans. This particular discovery, from the Olduvai Gorge, Tanzania, East Africa, dates from approximately 14,000,000 million years ago. It is apparently a grave of a socially high-ranking Ramapithecus, containing the complete mummified leftovers of a male, short of stature but impressively long on body parts associated with sex. "Ram", it seems, was buried with several females, all with curious smiles frozen on their desiccated faces. Bone analysis confirmed that Ram died of exhaustion. Cause of death in the females has not been established. Although the evidence is slim, it certainly appears as if science may be way wrong about its long-held modern belief (not including the feminist movement) that desire to please a mate sexually is a recent evolutionary phenomena. Note: This one discovery also began to bring into question the sincerity of oft-preferred assurances by females that size doesn't matter.

Since humans have apparently reproduced all through their history, and since it is a hard scientific fact that humans reproduce sexually today (if at all), and since "indoors" is a somewhat recent invention, many "sexperts" conclude that humans have a rich history of sex in the outdoors. But let's look at the facts. Archeologists have unearthed many artistic, and frankly pornographic, reproductions of human sexual activity. These discoveries, however, virtually all come from past metropolitan centers of civilization, i.e., cities, with the exception of a few crude, inconclusive cave-drawings here and there. Very little actual evidence exists to support the hypothesis that there has been a "rich history" of sex in the outdoors. It is much more believable that the sex acts pictured in those ancient reproductions (see National Geographic Magazine) were practiced only in pockets of humans as an aberration of normal behavior, and those pockets of humans, given what is evident today, quickly became cities. Perhaps sex in the outdoors back then was just too dangerous to be a common everyday occurrence. Perhaps the danger of exposure to a harsh environment and/or the danger of exposing one's position to a potential enemy were too great for a lot of sex to take place outdoors. After all, those same dangers exist today. The best that can be scientifically stated is this: Nobody knows for sure. But life is full of uncertainties, and these uncertainties have made research for this book a whole lot more interesting.

To bring the history of sex in the outdoors a bit closer to home, let's take a look at eastern Massachusetts, shortly after the arrival of the Pilgrims. Before escaping from the religious intolerance of England, and what with it being the pre-Industrial Revolution era, the Pilgrims, at least the wayward ones, most assuredly had some experience with rural sex (there were, after all, baby Pilgrims), but not with true sex in the outdoors as it is understood today. The first written record of any European's involvement in true sex in the outdoors comes from the splinter group, called Puritans, who moved up the coast to Salem some years after the landing at Plymouth Rock. (Note: Pre-Puritan sexual innuendoes, such as Leif Ericson's blond-haired blue-eyed influence on Canadian Eskimos and Columbus' contribution to the transatlantic distribution of certain viruses and bacteria, come to the pages of history through legend and not the written word.) From Salem the wilderness, the true outdoors, was close at hand . . . approximately 100 yards. Occasionally, couples would accidentally find themselves outdoors, usually on a Saturday, the day allotted for reproduction of the species. Since it was Saturday, and the Puritans were creatures of habit, these few attempted to reproduce the species and, in so doing, made a fascinating discovery, namely that sex in the outdoors, unlike the quiet cloistered sex of town, could be fun. The town fathers, being well-versed in intolerance, adept at voyeurism, and more than a little jealous, recognized the giggling as a real and present threat to their well-ordered society. So, as not to over-educate the people, the term "witchcraft" was conjured up as euphemism for sex in the outdoors. The subsequent fatal dunkings and burnings-at-the-stake effectively eliminated an entire class of budding sex-in-the-outdoors intelligentsia and negatively influenced public opinion concerning sex for years and years to come. In fact, that influence is still felt today. It was not until centuries later, after Kevin Costner filmed "Dances With Wolves", that white folks once again learned what most Native Americans always knew about the joys of sex in the outdoors.

Definition from the 1898 Universal Dictionary of the English Language: SEX. s. [Fr. sexe, from Latin sexum, accus. of sexus = sex, prob. lit. = a division, from seco = to cut. Spanish & Portuguese sexo, Italian sesso.]

I. Ordinary Language.
    1. The distinction between male and female; the physical difference between male and female; that property or character by which an animal is male or female. Sexual distinctions are derived from the presence and development of the characteristic generative organs of the male and female respectively.
    2. Womankind, by way of emphasis. (Generally preceded by the definite article "the.")
    3. One of the two divisions of animals founded on the distinction between male and female.

II. Botanical Language.
A distinctive peculiarity of some flower or flowers, as bearing a stamen or stamens, and therefore being analogous to the male sex in animals, or bearing a pistil or pistils, and thus being analogous to the female sex.

As one can see by this 100-year old definition, sex just always was . . . but just what it was was not very clearly defined. With the plants, writers courageously used terms bordering on turn-of-the-century botanical pornography, terms such as "pistil" and "stamen", but with animals, i.e., humans, they wimped out with "characteristic generative organs" to describe sex. "Sex" was apparently not a word describing a performance, something that someone actually did, until later in this century, although most everybody assuredly had an interest in fooling around. If this book had been written by Charles Dickens, it would probably have been entitled: How to Have Characteristic Generative Organ Contact in the Outdoors. Undoubtedly, it, too, would have been a bestseller.

In 1983, a group of outdoor-oriented physicians in California founded the Wilderness Medical Society. WMS is dedicated to " . . . serving the medical interests of the outdoor and wilderness community" and now has thousands of members. Unfortunately, both Masters and Johnson live in the Midwest, were not among the founding fathers and/or mothers of WMS, and have had no noticeable influence on the Society. Despite the obvious need for one, the Wilderness Medical Society has no Standing Committee on Sex in the Wilderness. Its research-based Journal of Wilderness Medicine offers a quarterly dose of mind-expanding articles such as this: "Monoclonal antibody detection of Giardia lamblia cysts in human stool by direct immunofluorescence." If the outdoor experts are wanting to dip their hands into relevant research, how about a little sex in the outdoors instead of shit.

As one can see, the history of sex in the outdoors lies shadowed by passive avoidance and/or active squelching of useful information. There does exist, however, a voluptuous body of knowledge gleaned from first, second and third hand reports that shed some light on this most fascinating subject. Much of this knowledge is contained within the pages of the book you hold in your hands. May it throw some light into the shadows.

Why Have Sex
in the Outdoors?

"Do bears poop in the woods? You bet. But that's not all they do!"
Smokey the Bear.

More and more people are striving toward a closer relationship
with the wild and good green earth that birthed all life (and, just as a
reminder, the prelude to all life is sex). Henry David Thoreau and

John Muir wanna-be's across this great land understand instinctively, on a gut level, that humanity has moved too far from its wilderness roots. Green individuals by the millions are actively seeking to reverse this trend by spending spare moments, weekends, and extended periods of time in the outdoors. This process of reconnecting to the natural world entails becoming familiar with one's natural activities in a wilderness setting so that the things one does naturally indoors become things one does naturally outdoors. At its best, sex in the outdoors should be exceptionally normal. At its very best, sex in the outdoors should be normally exceptional. The point is this: Since sex is normal, sex in the outdoors should be normal. It's time to get sex out from underneath the covers and back in the open where it belongs.

An Expression of Oneness with Nature

Sex is a many splendored thing. One of the splendored things sex in the outdoors can be is an expression of oneness with nature, perhaps the most beautiful expression. Like most species, humans have evolved naturally into a physical shape that lends itself to sex. Almost every other species on this earth does "the wild thing" in the natural world, i.e., outdoors, and some of them are doing it somewhere right now, even as you sit reading this compendium of silly knowledge about it. If you really want to re-establish your active membership in the brotherhood and sisterhood of all fauna (and flora, for that matter), you should be having sex in the outdoors. Next time you're doing "it" in the outdoors, think of your act as a ceremonial rite, a bonding of yourself to the natural world. Let yourself contact the rhythm of the universe through the rhythmic movement of your personal dance with nature. Let yourself feel, through your emotional high, the threads connecting you to the cosmos. Let yourself join, through your coming together, the fertile continuum of all life (even if you've decided to put a stopper in your own personal fertility).

An Expression on Oneness with another Oneness

Since it is impossible for any two people to draw physically closer together than when they have sex, it has been argued that there is no greater expression of oneness between a twoness than sex. If you're already into feeling universal rhythms and cosmic threads because you're outdoors, then this expression of oneness with another oneness should, understandably, reach new highs. Of course, it can be also be argued that sex in the indoors can be just as expressive . . . but the view isn't as good.

An Expression of Ecosensitivity

For those individuals with a growing sense of concern about humanity as a destructive force among fragile ecosystems, and for those whose concern has led to an inclination toward preservation of dwindling wild lands, it may be helpful to realize that sex in the outdoors can be a most expressive way to show ecosensitivity. In fact, sex in the outdoors may be the most environmentally sound activity in which one can engage while in pristine wilderness areas. Strip poker, for example, is far less disruptive than strip mining. (Note: There is that one notable exception from Montana in the early '60s where an entire tract of virgin forest bordering a hippie commune was decimated in a single night. It is exceptions, however, that make the rules!) Despite claims from the ecofringe crowd, there is absolutely no evidence that sex in the outdoors contributes to acid rain in any manner whatsoever. Neither does it have a detrimental effect on the ozone (with the exception, once again, of that one night in Montana). No other species has ever been pushed to extinction by human sex in the outdoors, nor has another species even been endangered . . . although a few have admittedly been embarrassed. (Note: More information about embarrassed species may be obtained from the US Department of Agriculture. Ask for the Embarrassed Species List.) If one chooses location and technique carefully, and observes a few basic rules of etiquette, long-term alteration of watersheds and weather patterns can be avoided, and the creation and distribution of toxic wastes can be eliminated (see Etiquette). Remember: Only you can prevent forest fires!

A New Dimension

For many city folk, there's something mysterious and fascinating about those people who go wandering into the wild places. Those of you who are among the wanderers-in-wild-places, and who also could use an additional dimension to your dull and in-desperate-need-of-an-improved-image sex life, consider this: There are possibly millions of would-be partners in the cities, fascinated by the mystique surrounding you (even though you know better), who just might be snookered into a foray into the wild. This very same person, who rolls his or her eyes behind your back when you make those tired, predictable, city-fied come-on's in the office may thrill to the suggestion of a moonlight hike up Pike's Peak. Somehow, it triggers a different response than your offer of a midnight stroll through Central Park . . . unarmed. Opening Line to Remember: "How 'bout we go down on, er, I mean, to the Wildlife Preserve this weekend, Doris?"

The corollary to the above idea is this: Sex in the outdoors can also bring an added dimension to your otherwise wild but increasing-difficult-to-maintain-the-image-of sex life. For those who expend lots of energy creating and maintaining a grandiose public image of their sex life, there's always the danger of running out of material. You can only relate so many variations on your urban/suburban sexual experiences to fellow travelers on the subway before the crowd starts to yawn. Outdoor sexual scenarios, on the other hand, are virtually limitless and offer, additionally, the aura of the exotic and/or primitive. Even a mediocre story-teller can get great mileage out of the wilderness milieu. After all, how many people actually know how far it is up Pike's Peak?

As Therapy?
The great vices of today seem to be: 1) Struggling to be on time, 2) Struggling to make the best use of time, and 3) Struggling in a brief span of time to "achieve" and "succeed." What all this struggling produces is unhappiness, lack of peace, disassociation and, finally, in the extreme, a bundle of psychotic disorders. But what a dynamic combo sex and the outdoors can be to reduce stress and improve one's self image! Ah, the healing power of the natural world combined with the healing power of the sex act. You may find here the ultimate therapeutic effect. Of course, many people have found this tack never works, but, hey, it's worth a try. Opening Line to Remember: "Let's go out to the national park, baby, and we can both reduce a little stress!"

Warning! Warning!

There is a force that draws thousands of people to the dark side of sex in the outdoors. Many people walk that thin line which separates fun and fanaticism. Sex in the outdoors can be habit forming. In fact, sex in the outdoors can be addicting. If you become hooked, outdoor sex can unravel the social fabric into which your days are woven, disrupting your whole life. Moderation, as in all things, is strongly advised.

Signs of Sex-in-the-Outdoors Addiction Include:

1. Having constant thoughts of sex in the outdoors (e.g., where should I go next?, should I bring a tent or a tarp?) to the point where the thoughts disrupt your work and your relationships.
2. Having to have sex in the outdoors regularly to maintain a personal sense of well-being.
3. Being overwhelmed by physiological and psychological depression if you don't have sex in the outdoors regularly (a.k.a. withdrawal).
4. Having to have sex in the outdoors more and more often (i.e., progressively larger doses) to achieve the desired effects.
5. Having sex in the outdoors to excess, so you're exhausted and hung over on Monday morning.
6. Leaving your Chicago office early so you can have sex in the Boundary Waters Canoe Area on your way home to Merrillville, Indiana.
7. Hiding trees in your bedroom.

Management of the Patient includes:

1. Explaining in a calm, quiet manner to the patient of sex-in-the-outdoors overdose and/or withdrawal that you are there to help. Remember, even though the patient may be acting irrationally and/or inappropriately, he or she is almost always very frightened.
2. Maintaining eye contact, but not looking at any other body parts.
3. Wearing protective gloves, goggles and mask if there is any chance of contacting the patient's body fluids.
4. Protecting yourself from attack by the patient.
5. Gathering as much information as possible (e.g., when the patient last had sex in the outdoors, how often does he or she regularly do "it", routes of administration, which geographic areas) in case you have to refer the patient to professional help.

Note: Sex In The Woods Anonymous (SITWA) chapters are opening up all across the United States. For the address and phone number of the chapter nearest you, contact: SITWA National Office, 198 Kearsage, North Conway, NH 03860.

Preparation Be Fore Play

"An ounce of preparation is worth a pound of Blackberry Love Liquor." Benjamin Franklin Jones.

Spontaneity may arguably be the greatest source of enjoyment. There's nothing like a little well-planned spontaneity to improve sex in the outdoors. Remember the "Six P's": Prior Planning Prevents Piss-Poor Performance. Forethought may prove almost as valuable as foreplay.

Equipment

When preparing for most outdoor trips, packing right means packing light. Who wants to waste a lot of valuable energy carrying too much weight? Excuse to Avoid: "Not tonight, Melvin, I'm just too tired!" Choose a small backpack. When it's full, a clear sign has been given that enough stuff has been packed. Distribution of gear between partners is significant since weight-bearing carries an importance of its own. Rubbing shoulders tired from the load of a pack often leads to rubbing more interesting body parts. Packing light may safely be ignored when planning many water-based adventures, but, don't forget, shoulders often need rubbing after a day of wielding a paddle. Opening Line to Remember: "I once took a course in massage therapy."

Shelter (The Sex Was In Tents):

Laying out under the stars has a lot going for it, if environmental conditions are conducive, but never leave civilization without a tent. Tents are insurance, providing protection from wind, rain, snow, sun, cold, insects, arachnids, most wild mammals, and Peeping Toms. A candle lantern fills the fabric-walled bedroom with a soft, romantic glow. A well-placed campfire, when appropriate, flickers delightfully through the bright-colored nylon. Tarps give some insurance, but not enough. Carry a tent.

Choose a tent that sets up quickly and easily. Practice setting up a

new tent at home to prevent frustration in case spontaneity raises its grinning face. How devastating to find the mood shattered by one's inability to fit the appropriate pole into the correct slot. But no matter how easily it sets up always consider asking for assistance. Setting up the tent may be a shared experience that has a chance to provide a subtle basis for a later and decidedly more intimate shared experience.

Free-standing tents are obviously the best choice. They can be set up in almost any terrain, and there's no tight lines to fall over when you slip out for a pee. (Note: A self-deploying tent, like a self-inflating sleeping pad, would be a terrific piece of gear, something wonderfully advantageous should a sudden urge strike.) And don't pick a tent that's too small. Plenty of room should be available for rolling around inside. When choosing a tent, consideration should be given to favored sexual positions. Who wants to be constrained by lack of space? On second thought, consider all sexual positions. Who wants to be constrained? Solo shelters are generally unacceptable. Huge basecamp tents are okay for group sex.

Sleeping Bags:
Whoever thought of zip-together sleeping bags should be awarded the Nobel Prize for Outdoor Sex. Whoever travels into the outdoors with mismatched sleeping bags is not dedicated to achieving a maximal sexual experience. Excuse to Avoid: "Margaret, that cold draft turns me off!" For those who haven't noticed, the whole of the space within zip-together bags is greater than the sum of their individual spaces. Excuse to Avoid: "That won't work, Merv . . . there's not enough room!" In some cases, ending up with bags that zip together may require creative thinking: "OK, you bring the wine, and I'll bring the bags." Or: "Did you know I got two sleeping bags this year for Christmas? We might as well use them, and you can leave your old one at home."

The loft of the bags, i.e. how much body heat they retain, should be appropriate to the season, but not too appropriate. If you anticipate sharing some heated moments, always opt for a bag with a little less loft than the expected ambient air temperature would indicate. Opening Line to Remember: "I think you'd be warm enough if we snuggled."

Sleeping Pads:
Proper choice of sleeping pads rates nearly as close to critical as proper choice of sleeping bags. Standard air mattresses are simply too great a risk. They may deflate at the most inconvenient moment or, even worse, pop and eliminate all immediate hope for comfort. For old-fashioned outdoorspersons, closed-cell foam pads will do. More up-to-date outdoor enthusiasts will choose, instead, a couple of modern, rugged, self-inflating pads that give a wide margin for safety as well as adequate padding from rough, hard, cold ground. These, too, by the way, are available in models that attach to each other, insurance against a sudden shift in comfort.

The truly dedicated always carry a third pad, leaving out less essential items . . . such as food. Third pads will serve one of two purposes: 1) It can fill up the extra space in the tent for those who really roll around a lot, and 2) It can be added where pressure points exist, e.g. under the hips, for extra warmth and comfort. Excuse to Avoid: "I'm sorry, Myrtle . . . I just can't find a comfortable position!" (Note: Fanatics have been known to carry four sleeping pads.)

Despite the labels "sleeping" bag and "sleeping" pad, whether one actually sleeps or not is another consideration altogether.

Clothing:

Once outdoor clothing resulted exclusively from the weaving of natural fibers, and came in drab color choices of dark earthy tones. Clothing today consists primarily of long chains of petroleum molecules in colors described by long chains of fabulous words, e.g. Tortugan Parrot-Feather, East African Sunset, Brazilian Rainforest. For the outdoor sexual enthusiast, the important considerations once were: Am I protected from the environment? and Will this stuff come off easily when I no longer want to be protected? (Note: If things work out, and the other person is taking your clothing off you, your outdoor wear should be a challenge to remove but not a hardship.) Although these are still important points to consider, today the additional question is asked: Do I look good? This is not an inconsequential question if you have to get the attention of a potential partner. In many species, and increasingly so with humans, it is the "best dressed" individual that attracts the mate.

Confusion mounts as the customer must choose clothing to match the intended outdoor pursuit. So speaks the salesperson: "A pile sweater? Will you be backpacking, mountain biking, canoeing, rockclimbing, high altitude mountaineering, cross country skiing, kayaking, or trying to pick up a date at the Boulder Mall?" Excuse to Avoid: "I like you, Martin, but your fuchsia GoreTex shorts clash with your scarlet capilene longjohns!"

Fortunately, the accepted dress for the sex act itself has changed little with the ages.

Food And Wine:

Traditionally, an enjoyable meal has been a preface to sex. A few pre-trip questions about what the other person likes would certainly be appropriate, but here are several suggestions: 1) Choose foods that are at least politically correct. Imagine opening a can of tuna to display parts of a dead fish that was caught in a net! There goes the evening. 2) Choose foods from the category marked "aphrodisiac", e.g. oysters, onions, tomatoes, cherries, cherry tomatoes, bananas, fish (including eels), broad beans and green M&Ms. Season everything with hot spices, except the M&Ms. (Note: Playing with your food, e.g. hide-and-seek the cherry, can be a great way to break the ice.) 3) Don't eat too much. Excuse to Avoid: "I can't, Marge . . . I'm too full!" 4) Carry foods that can be licked off your partner, e.g., jam, honey, syrup, whipped cream, bacon grease (for devoted carnivores). And 5) Don't drink too much alcohol. A cup of wine heightens interest and mellows mood. Too much firewater and the water puts out the fire.

Note: There are indications that you've had too much alcohol to drink. For instance, if you can't remember if your partner had an orgasm or not, you've probably had too much to drink. If you can't remember if you've had an orgasm or not, you've definitely had too much to drink. If you can't remember who your partner is, you've had way too much to drink. If you can't remember who you are, you should see a doctor . . . soon. If you've lost interest in having sex, you're an alcoholic. Puking is another bad sign.

Improvisation:
One is limited only by one's imagination. No shelter? Crawl under

some deadfall or into a cave. No sleeping pad? Rake some leaves and pine needles together. No sleeping bag? Use your clothes. No food? Go hungry. In the spirit of our forefathers and foremothers, who challenged and tamed the outdoors, and who obviously had sex — how else could they be fathers and mothers? — do not be denied by the lack of a few amenities. Where there's a will, there's a way! Excuse to Avoid: "Oh, no, I forgot the . . . . !"

Sexual Adjuncts:
Here personal preference is the only guiding factor, but, remember, the ability to improvise is one of the greatest signs of someone who is truly skilled in sex in the outdoors. Vegetable oil, as an example, has many uses.

Physical Fitness
Many people put hours and hours into choosing and packing the right gear and food while forgetting that the basic piece of equipment for sex in the outdoors is made of flesh and blood. As with any outdoor adventure, your body needs to be honed for sex. Lack of physical preparation may lead to pooping out before the fun really begins. Signs of poor fitness include 1) Saying you have a desire to watch the sunset when the truth is you don't have the energy to crawl into the tent, and 2) Getting breathless while undressing. As a guideline, the International Council on Outdoor Sexual Fitness says that if you feel the need to lie down and rest after locking your car at the trailhead, you're probably in less than adequate physical condition.

Endurance Training:
Any of the cardiovascular exercises, e.g., walking, jogging, swimming, biking, will do the most for overall conditioning for sex in the outdoors. These types of exercises will allow you to keep going longer. Holding your breath while doing these exercises will really help you prepare for prolonged sexual experiences.

Strength Training:
A few push-ups and sit-ups, several of each several times a week, will help keep you in shape for general strength needs during outdoor sex, such as rolling over and shaking your partner until he or she wakes up. Some people find muscle-specific strength training

exercises valuable, such as squeezing a basketball between your knees until you are able to pop it, and peeling a banana using only your lips and tongue. Don't overdo it!

Flexibility Training:
Everyone should be able to lean over and touch their toes, or at least their knees, in order to maintain enough flexibility to prevent damage to muscles and ligaments during sex. In addition, becoming more flexible will allow you to attempt more fascinating things during sexual activity. Encourage your partner to stay in shape, too.

Mental Fitness
A lot of people have lost sight of the fact that the mind and the body are one. You can keep your body ready, but your mind can lose interest. Prayer and meditation are time-honored ways to keep your mind in shape. More recent mind-conditioning methods include biofeedback, psychotherapy, neurolinguistic programming, self-hypnosis and herbal teas. Consider packing in a XXX-rated book.

Special Techniques for Special Places

"It is during sex that our bodies do, or at least try to do, the most magical and wonderful things. We grab and grope, slide and squirm, reach and stretch, strain our muscles and perform feats of agility that would flabbergast an ape." Richard Smith in The Dieter's Guide to Weight Loss During Sex.

21

When the going gets tough, the intelligent go someplace else . . . where the going isn't so tough. One the greatest reasons, however, for the survival of humans as a species is probably the ability of humans to figure out how to make do with situations when there simply aren't any immediate alternatives. "Special Techniques for Special Places" is a celebration of human adaptability and perseverance. One who successfully attempts to do "it" in a "special" place does so for the obvious reason . . . which is, naturally, the chance to brag about an heroic act performed against insurmountable odds under extremely adverse conditions.

High Angle Sex

For those who enjoy the vertical world — finger jams, sewing-machine legs, desperate moves with poor protection — the term "safe sex" takes on a whole new meaning. First, as with all outdoor pursuits, choice of companions is the prime predictor of success. The climber must find an acceptable partner whose lead can be followed or who can follow the lead. What good are lofty thoughts of sex when you and the object of your desire end up separated by 165 feet of 11 mm perlon? Excuse to Avoid: "Sorry, Elwood, this pitch won't go for me!"

Next, the climber must be very sure of the quality of the equipment he or she has chosen and the security of the anchors he or she has placed. Now clip in one of those tidy little nylon bedrooms, one that has a cover for privacy, the one that has been hanging all day in a haul bag at the end of the rope. Views tend to be grand, but are often best avoided. The next move is the crux — getting out of harnesses, out of clothes, back into harnesses without falling to an untimely-but-undoubtedly-much-publicized death. Before getting down to business, check to make sure you are both secured to tethers of a length appropriate to allow the deed. Hopefully, you are both wearing harnesses that won't get in the way . . . too much. Practice at home prior to attempts on a vertical face is strongly suggested. Opening Lines to Consider: "Don't worry, I've done this before!"

Being, for the most part, afraid of heights, I have had to rely on firsthand accounts from friends who have a better sense of balance and less fear. My favorite story is from El Capitan's Salathe Wall, where the evening assault was on a noted female climber. During the act, he said, she had unbuckled the leg straps of her harness, and a shift in the hanging platform shoved her waistbelt up to her armpits. The deformation of her chest, she said, was alarming. I don't remember if they made the summit or not.

Laying while Belaying

For those who can't wait till bedtime, or who think the thrill would justify the risk, some belay points offer an opportunity for sex in the outdoors. Ledges are considered the most acceptable, but, hey, any port in a storm. Discretion is advised. Excuse to Avoid: "You're not clipped in!" Excuse to Accept: "No way, Eleanor. If we botch this, we die!"

Once again, I turn to a friend of mine who claims that, in a rash act of spontaneity, nine months before the birth of her first child, she found love on a ledge, with several extremities hanging over the void, a most exhilarating experience.

Going Down Below Ground

The cave's a fine and private place, but few there are that there embrace. Caves offer the possibility of some advantages, e.g. silence, privacy, the dramatic echoes in an underground cavern, squirming through snug passageways has made you both horny and there's noboby else around. Caves also provide some disadvantages. They are chilly, damp, dirty, and infinitely dark. "It is not the darkness I fear," whispered Elmer, "it is what the darkness hides." Comfortable dry bedding, a thermos of hot coffee laced with whisky, and adequate lighting may provide an opportunity for an unusual sexual experience. Excuse to Avoid: "I knew you were down there somewhere, Elsie, but I couldn't find you."

As with heights, I have no great fondness for caves, and I'm often heard echoing the words of the chronicler of old: "There is time enough for the earth in the grave." There is something weird, to my mind, about those people who go underground voluntarily before they are dead. My information comes from a caving instructor friend who claims to have been in many tight places in caves of the Midwest.

The Rush of Swift Water

Ever bounce along on a rubber raft through Class III and IV water, looking at the way some of the other scantily-clad rafters are bouncing along, feeling the warm sun put an itch in your britches?

Ever wonder what it would be like to intimately share the bouncing? Like a waterbed, perhaps, but carried to a daredevilish degree. Here are several suggestions: 1) Do not remove personal flotation devices (PFDs). 2) Do not try this without a third, understanding companion who is competent and willing to maintain control of the raft. 3) Do your part to keep the raft upright by striving to cooperate with the oarsperson and thrust yourself into the oncoming waves. You don't want to end up rolling in the haystacks. Excuse to Avoid: "I can't swim!"

I saw this first on the lower San Juan River of southeastern Utah. Magnificent sandstone edifices rose from both banks of the turbulent yellow water. A brilliant April sun warmly filled a soft blue sky. It was a large raft, and more than one understanding companion was ogling the act. I sat taking a break from paddling my canoe, stretched on a riverside dune of white sand. As the raft flowed past, I realized what I was seeing and looked away . . . as soon as they were far enough downriver for the detail to be lost through my binoculars.

Swamp Thing

Extensive marshy areas offer days of wandering narrow wet passages through geographic regions without a single square foot of solid ground. Canoes are the only crafts small and maneuverable enough to allow access while providing an acceptable-but-tippy base for overnighting. One learns to excrete body wastes while balanced delicately over the gunwale, to cook with the stove balanced delicately on a thwart, and to do other-but-more-satisfying things while balanced delicately. Here are some suggestions: 1) Place unneeded gear in a waterproof bag, tie off the bag, and let it float beside the canoe during the night. 2) Keep your centers of gravity low. 3) Plan shifts in position well in advance.

I remember one night in Florida . . . the moon almost full, a gentle breeze keeping the mosquitoes down while carrying the scents of sawgrass and palm, the chitter of nightbirds and the bark of alligators. I wish I could say more, but that's all I remember . . . I was alone. I wish I could brag of heroic acts performed against insurmountable odds under extremely adverse conditions

Environmental Exposure

"Although nature and natural causes be forced and resisted ever so much, yet at last they will have their own way again." George Best.

Hypothermia

As a species, humans evolved on the savannahs of Africa for a very good reason . . . it's real warm there. Few, if any, historians recognize the role cold has played in human evolution. Even in the hairiest moments of human pre-history, Homo sapiens were never adequately prepared to deal with cold. When the earth started to cool down planetwide, early humans were required to take the hairy skins from other species and wear them to make up for their own evolutionary inadequacies. To take hair from other pre-historic creatures necessitated, of course, the taking of their lives as well. (Note: Volunteerism never became very popular until the Republican Party came along.) Not many people today realize that this was the original Cold War. Early humans also discovered a satisfaction that came from the act of killing, whether they needed hair, or food, and they passed that satisfaction on to all future generations. Thus, cold became the progenitor of Regular War, and murder, and, even now, humans speak of unkind fellow humans as being "cold-hearted" or "cold-blooded."

Millenia passed and humans learned other ways to help themselves survive in the cold. They learned, for instance, that laying around on the ground was not as warm as laying around on the hairy skins of other animals. So, beds were invented . . . another example of how cold has led to destruction of other life-forms. The invention of beds soon led to the discovery that snuggling on one with another pre-human was warmer than sleeping alone. Snuggling naturally led to sex because the "act" produced lots more heat than simple snuggling. Thus, cold led directly to sex in the outdoors as a sport rather than something done only to reproduce the species. Later it was discovered that other things improved sex in the outdoors, such as a roaring fire and strong wine, and, as a by-product, it was noted that fire and wine also helped one cope with the cold.

Humans who did not learn to cope with the cold died. It was said, once language was created, that they had died from "exposure" of the outside of their bodies to low temperatures. This was true until the 1950s when hypothermia — getting too cold on the inside of the body — was invented at a doctor's convention in New Orleans. The doctors were convening in New Orleans because physicians have historically had difficulty coping with cold, which is why hospital thermostats are always set around 100 degrees F. Undoubtedly, millions of people would have died from hypothermia if it had been invented sooner.

Today hypothermia rates, understandably, as one of the greatest risks to the health and safety of those who pursue sex in the outdoors. It also rates as one of the greatest deterrents to sex in the outdoors. Prevention is all-important. Excuse to Avoid: "Nosirree! It's too cold!"

Prevention of Hypothermia:
1. Shelter. To prevent hypothermia, some form of shelter is highly recommended. Originally, shelter was caves, and they still work today. In some regions, caves are hard to find, but tents are more than adequate (see chapter on Preparation Be Fore Play). It is best to secure a shelter before moving to the next step in prevention.
2. Fuel for the Human Engine. A quiet dinner for two is in order. Carbohydrates, tastefully spiced, burn more easily, providing quicker heat and energy. If this meal can be cooked and eaten within the heat of a campfire, hypothermia is even more prevented. If a campfire is inappropriate, at least have a candle.
3. Fluids. Although water works best as the fluid to drink for the

prevention of hypothermia, wine should not be overlooked. First, the mellowing effect of the alcohol makes the human brain less aware of cold and, therefore, helps prevent excuses (see above). Second, alcohol causes peripheral vasodilation which is why skin gets warm and reddish. Vasodilated skin aids in the transfer of heat from the outside of the body to the inside, an important consideration in the prevention of hypothermia once snuggling begins. Furthermore, vasodilated skin has a heightened sensitivity to touch. Opening Lines to Remember: "Just one drink, Suzanne. It helps prevent hypothermia!" (Note: Although wine is the traditional drink associated with sex in the outdoors, other forms of alcohol may work just as well.) Excessive consumption of alcohol is definitely not recommended since it can destroy the mood as well as one's ability to find the tent.

4. Clothing. To prevent hypothermia, clothing should be loose-fitting and bulky. Loose-fitting in order to slip out of it quickly and easily so you're not over-exposed to the cold for very long. Bulky in order to stuff it around, under and/or over you to hold in body heat. (Note: The key word to remember when dressing for the outdoors is "layering". Layering means you are dressed to allow for comfortable laying in a variety of climes.)

5. Pacing. Pacing is critical in hypothermia prevention for two reasons: 1) Overwork uses up energy stores, leaving you too exhausted to continue producing heat (as well as too exhausted to continue). 2) Overwork makes you sweaty, and you must stay dry to stay warm.

6. Adjusting to Extremes. Since the nature of sex in the outdoors inherently tends toward heat and sweat, allowances can be made by adjusting to these extremes. This is perhaps simpler than it sounds. When you feel yourself getting hot and sweaty, unzip the sleeping bags and throw off the excess coverings, i.e. bulky clothing. When you feel yourself getting chilled, zip up the bags and pull the excess coverings back over you.

Since hypothermia first and foremost reduces one's ability to think clearly, despite the most profound precautions, you may find yourself responsible for the care of a hypothermic companion. It may prove fortunate that sex in the outdoors, in addition to being a risk, has long been recognized as a treatment for hypothermia.

Treatment of Hypothermia:
1. Active External Rewarming. This is sometimes known as the Cuddle Technique. For maximum treatment, both parties should be naked and as much skin as possible on the normothermic person should be in contact with as much skin as possible on the hypothermic person. Don't forget that a cup of wine helps maximize skin-to-skin heat

transfer. Both parties should be bundled in as much insulation as possible, including insulation from the cold ground, and care should be taken to make sure there are no leaks in the bundling where Cold Monsters can sneak in and take a bite. If zip-together sleeping bags are being used (a great advantage), a third normothermic person can be added to the treatment, but the third person should be someone you know really well.

2. Active Internal Rewarming. This is sometimes known as the Copulation Technique. Follow the recommendations for Active External Rewarming with the addition of blatant sex. Care must be taken to monitor the patient for the Sexual Thermodynamic Reversal Phenomenon which states that, physiologically, it is easier to cool down a human than to warm one up unless sex is added and then it is easier to warm up a human than to cool one down. In the case of the thermodynamically unstable human, this warming up process may produce excessive heat which could be a problem. It is strongly recommended that the care provider start slow and build gradually toward a climax of heat production.

Frostbite

Unlike hypothermia, in which the whole body gets cold, frostbite happens when the cold takes a bite out of a localized area of the body. During sex this happens because one's mind is somewhere else. It happens most often to toes, that somehow ended up sticking out of the sleeping bag, or the butt, for the same reason. (Note: The expression "I froze my butt off!" originally came from a sexual experience near Gunnison, Colorado, in 1853 when Captain Gunnison's troops first encountered, simultaneously, extreme winter conditions and Ute maidens.) Other body parts can be involved, especially if you fall asleep exhausted and carelessly covered. Frostbitten parts can be recognized because they will be pale and numb . . . unlike the rest of the body. Treatment for frostbite should be immediate and gentle skin-to-skin contact. Opening Line to Remember: "It's looks like frostbite to me, Sluggo!"

Hyperthermia

Although the risk is low, it is generally accepted among the experts that certain predisposed individuals can become too hot — hyperthermic — while having sex in the outdoors. At special risk would be those individuals who hadn't had "any" for a long, long time. Environmental conditions to consider avoiding, in order to prevent hyperthermia, would be direct sunlight when the ambient air temperature is high and the humidity is almost as high. For example, Florida during the daylight hours should be considered a high risk region for sex in the outdoors, which is why there are more air-conditioned motel rooms than private homes in the Sunshine State. Hyperthermia should, however, be thought of as a serious threat to one's sex life, and treatment should be appropriate.

Treatment of Hyperthermia:

Cooling off the patient is the only effective treatment. After moving the patient to a shady spot, remove all clothing, if this hasn't already been done. Fanning and massaging are effective means of cooling, especially if the patient's skin has been wet beforehand. If ice is available, it can be rubbed gently over the patient's skin, especially in areas of the body where ice is seldom rubbed. Care must be taken to avoid cooling the patient too rapidly, which has been known to produce heat.

Sunburn

Sunshine produces more potential problems than just heat — ultraviolet radiation, for instance. It's the ultraviolet radiation (UVR) that causes sunburn. UVR takes time to burn human skin, so it probably won't mess up your first sex-in-the-sun experience. But if you're planning a multi-day outdoor trip, e.g., beachcombing in Baja, you'll definitely want to take precautions in order to prevent Burned Buns Syndrome (BBS). BBS has been known to prevent sex. Precautions to prevent sex-in-the-sun-burn before it prevents sex include but are not limited to: 1) Doing it in the shade, which is possible on many lakeshores and some beaches, especially if you bring your own shade, e.g., a big umbrella. 2) Smearing a sunblock over everybody's entire body. Sunblocks let no UVR through, and include substances such as zinc oxide (ZO), which has the advantage of making you real slippery. Warning: Some people think being real slippery is not an advantage. ZO used to be available only in white, but now comes in brilliant colors. Warning: Some people find that a body entirely smeared with lime-green ZO is a turn-off. 3) Coating everybody's body with a sunscreen. Sunscreens allow you to expose yourself to the sun longer without being burned. Every sunscreen container is labeled with a Sex Promotion Factor (SPF), which tells you how much longer you can have sex in the sun. A screen of SPF 15, for example, allows you to have sex in the sun 15 times longer than if you are not wearing that particular screen. Some sunscreens wash off easily with water and/or sweat, so be sure to ask for sex-proof sunscreen.

High Altitude Illness

It is a well-known fact that the higher one goes above sea-level the less oxygen there is to breathe. This produces a condition known as hypoxia, which means low-oxygen. Hypoxia has a direct and immediate effect on the brain, causing it to have less fun, a serious consideration if one intends to have sex at high altitude. In addition to having less fun, other signs and symptoms of altitude illness include headache, nausea, loss of appetite, unusual fatigue, insomnia (not necessarily a problem) and lassitude (a condition describing loss of interest in sex, a serious problem).

Prevention of High Altitude Illness:

1. Acclimatization. This is the single most important factor in preventing high altitude problems. Acclimatization is a process in which the human body adjusts, and thus is able to function normally, under hypoxic conditions. Although it takes weeks for the full benefits of acclimatization to take effect, everyone should be able to function relatively normally after a couple of days at any given altitude. Since exercise tolerance will be lower, start slow . . . maybe with kissing and petting only on the first day. For individuals who are gaining altitude

daily, i.e. high altitude mountaineers, it is strongly suggested that altitude be gained no faster than the body can acclimatize. There is a formula for figuring how fast altitude can be safely gained. It states that above 10,000 feet above sea-level, no one should sleep higher than 1000 feet above their previous night's sleeping altitude. This does not mean that you can't gain more than 1000 feet per day if you need, for instance, to ferry loads to a higher camp. It does mean that you should drop back down for the night. This is the source of the old mountaineering adage: "Climb high, have sex low." Excuse to Avoid: "I'm sorry, Hank . . . I really do have a headache!"

2. Fitness. Although fitness does not prevent altitude illness, it most definitely increases one's ability to acclimatize. If you are planning on having lots of sex at high altitude, you should obviously have lots at lower altitudes in preparation. Opening Lines to Remember: "Honestly, Harriet, I need this in order to train for my next climb!"

3. Drinking and Eating. Drinking lots of water and eating lots of food helps prevent altitude illness. This, too, can be practiced at lower altitude.

Treatment for Altitude Illness:

Descend, which, in this case, does not necessarily mean "go down."

Note: High altitude mountaineers who successfully attempt to have sex on the summit of the mountain they are climbing may qualify for membership in a small, prestigious and little-known club. The summit must be higher than 14,000 feet above sea-level and there must have been at least two climbers involved. Send your name, the name of the mountain, and vivid details of the experience to The Peak Experience, Box 9, Pitkin, Colorado 81241.

Phallic Shock

Although not common, incidents of phallic shock are well-documented, especially at high altitude, and should be considered before attempting sex. In phallic shock, the sudden rush of blood to the penis causes the victim to pass out. Treatment should include keeping the victim supine with his feet higher than his head (his hat-wearing head) and avoiding touching his penis. Prevention should include staying well-hydrated and letting things build up a bit slower. Deaths are rare.

Low Altitude Illness

This is sometimes referred to as Drowning, a condition occurring when sex is attempted in water by those who are ill-prepared for the attempt. Here are some suggestions: 1) Practice at home in a bathtub first. 2) Fly to Hawaii or a lush Caribbean island for your first in-the-outdoors experience. The water will be warm (a plus) and salt water is more buoyant than fresh water (another plus). 3) Wear a personal flotation device (PFD) or, better yet, snorkeling gear or, even better yet, SCUBA gear.

Further Precautions for Freshwater Sex: 1) In shallow freshwater, the sex act is well-documented to attract leeches . . . leeches of the non-human variety. Their presence often alters the mood of the moment dramatically. And any freshwater that provides a home for ducks and snails may also be home for a schistosome that is deposited on the water's bottom in duck and snail poo-poo. Thrashing around in shallow water can stir up the schistosomes allowing them to take up residence on human skin which causes a very uncomfortable dermatitis known as Swimming Sex-Itch. Keeping your freshwater sex in deep water will prevent the problems of leeches and itching. 2) In the Amazon River there lives a tiny fish that likes to swim up into and attach itself to human urethras. It works something like a heat-seeking missile. This problem, too, can be prevented by staying deep while having sex in the water.

Note: Reports from Alaska give evidence that it is possible to have sex in the water while wearing specially-designed wetsuits, but indications are it isn't worth the effort.

Treatment for Drowning:
Prolonged mouth-to-mouth breathing interspersed with chest compressions at a ratio of 2 full breaths to 15 compressions. For maximum benefit, both mouth and chest should be bare. Mouth-to-mouth breathing should be practiced regularly at home and in the outdoors. Chest compressions should be practiced, but only pretend to compress the chest.

Uninvited Guests and other Dangerous Critters

1. INSECTS (e.g. mosquitoes, ants, bees, wasps, no-see-ums, flies, redbugs, bedbugs, deadbugs). One of the things that almost everyone who pursues sex in the outdoors desires is privacy. One of the things that insects deny is privacy. And, for another thing, there is a lot of exposure to insects during outdoor sex. "Hazel, is that you crawling up my leg?" All insects have three characteristics in common: 1) They all have segmented bodies. 2) They all have six legs. 3) They all enjoy bothering humans. Many insects play an important role in the delicate balance of nature, but some do not. Take mosquitoes, for instance. There is absolutely no reason for a mosquito. Mosquitoes have ruined more outdoor sex than all other natural disasters combined.

There are three ways to avoid contact with most insects:
1) Go to places where insects aren't. This is more difficult and costly than it sounds, but trips to the North and South Pole have been increasing over the past decade. It is reasonable to assume many of these trips have been planned in order to seek uninterrupted sex in the outdoors (see Hypothermia).
2) Make sure your tent has no rips in it and that the zipper works on the mosquito netting over the door. The rule is: Zip before you unzip. If you accidentally leave the tent door open too long, you might be better off keeping it open until all the insects, e.g. mosquitoes, fly in, at which time you rush out and zip them up inside the tent, leaving you and your partner alone under the stars. Note: This requires perfect timing and is generally considered the second best plan.
3) Wear insex repellent. Insex repellent is any substance that repels insects while you're involved having sex. The newest innovation in a long line of insex repellents is a product that contains permethrin which, when allowed to soak into clothing, actually kills insects when

they try to crawl around on the clothing. The repellent, which is truly an insecticide, will not, say the experts, harm humans or dogs . . . but then the same words were once spoken about DDT. Permethrin will, obviously, not work, unless you are anticipating some well-clothed sex. Older products that contain DEET have been proven to repel insects. 25 to 35% concentrations of DEET will repel all insects, and some arachnids, i.e. ticks. DEET must go on skin, and a significant amount of it soaks in and disappears to somewhere inside the body. Both partners must choose to wear DEET because if only one opts for the repellent both end up wearing it anyway. Of course, liberal applications of lotions containing DEET can be fun and rewarding. Not nearly as effective as DEET is a product called Skin-So-Soft which is totally harmless (to humans and insects), smells nice, and rubs on pleasantly. Opening Line to Remember: "You don't want to miss any spots, Hal. The 'skeeters 'round here are terrible!"

2. ARACHNIDS (e.g. spiders, scorpions, ticks). Unlike insects, arachnids have eight legs and generally don't enjoy humans. Even ticks prefer mice and deer, and attach themselves to humans only when there is a shortage of other food sources. But, unlike most insects, the bites and stings of some arachnids can cause serious injury, devastating disease, and sometimes death.

Spiders to especially avoid are the female Black Widow (which may be brown but has an hourglass-shape on the underside of her abdomen) and both sexes of the Brown Recluse (which may be black but has a fiddle or violin-shape on the upperside of his or her head and back). Spiders normally roam around feeding at night, so stay in your tent as much as possible. Don't gather firewood in the dark, and don't wander outside barefoot and/or barebutt. Encounters with the fangs of these spiders are almost always painless, but excruciating pain comes in 20 minutes to an hour. The pain lasts a long time and effectively ruins the encounter you are after. Death is rare, so victims usually get to try again some other day. Leaving the outdoors to find a doctor is advised, but there is no rush. Male humans, however, are often bitten on their testicles by black widows when the human uses an outhouse that the spider has chosen for a home. These victims may not get to try again some other day. Rapidly leaving the outdoors to find a doctor is strongly advised. Painkillers and sedatives may be given to the patient.

Scorpions, like spiders, generally shun the light of day, and anti-spider precautions will work for scorpions, too. Scorpions do not bite, but, instead, sting with the tip of their abdomen, which looks like a curled up tail. The sting of any scorpion is universally and immediately painful, but the only sting that may lead to a human death, in the United States, comes from a slim, yellowish or greenish-colored resident of the desert Southwest. Scorpion stings are like a whopping beesting, and the pain goes away fairly soon. Cold applied to the site of the sting makes the pain go away sooner. Pain may ruin the moment, but not necessarily the whole event. If the patient, however, starts to feel sick and loses all interest in having sex, it is either 1) A result of the scorpion sting, or 2) A result of the atrocious smell from your polypropylene underwear combined with the unwashed condition of your body. In either case, you might as well leave the outdoors and seek help.

Ticks, worldwide, carry more diseases that humans can catch than anything except mosquitoes. They don't transmit disease by crawling around on human skin. They have to bury their heads and feed for awhile before germs are passed. It takes hours to days of feeding before enough germs are passed to make a human sick. Although some people seem to get quite sick when they find a tick creeping over their skin, that kind of sick doesn't count. Only fever, chills, nausea, achey joints and rashes count. When ticks are discovered already buried in, they should be removed immediately. Many methods of tick removal fill the pages of medical history, and most of them have a common characteristic — they don't work very well. For instance, heating up a tick's rear end with a recently-extinguished match makes the tick very angry, causing the little guy or gal to expel lots of germs before backing out. Smearing a thick ointment over the tick allows feeding to go on for a long time before he or she needs to come up for air. Grabbing the tick and twisting it counterclockwise (or is it clockwise?) very effectively screws off the tick's head and leaves germs in the patient's body. This is what works: Use tweezers to gently grasp the tick near the patient's skin and slowly pull it straight out. In order to remove all ticks before germs are passed, it is necessary to perform careful tick-checks two or three times a day. Ticks like best warm, moist, dark places on the human body, and tick-checks, as you might imagine, have led to much more interesting things. Opening Line to Remember: "Since you can't see down there, Helen, I'll check it for you!"

3. REPTILES (e.g. snakes, lizards). All snakes and most lizards should be considered dangerous because so many people have been hurt running away from them. Running away, incidentally, is the appropriate response. Not all snakes are poisonous. The ones that are, in the United States, are either Pit Vipers or Coral Snakes. Pit Vipers have slit, cat-like pupils and a heat-sensitive pit between eyes and nostrils. If you're close enough to see that, you deserve to be bitten. Some Pit Vipers have rattles and some do not. Coral Snakes have distinctly colored bands of red and yellow and black. "Red on black, venom lack, red on yellow, kill a fellow . . . or a woman." If you hear rattling, or see bands of bright color, or see a snake, or think a snake is nearby, run away. The only lizard in the US considered poisonous is the Gila Monster, which lives in a burrow in the Southwest near the dangerous scorpion. Gila Monsters are black and orange and bumpy. Reptiles are night-feeders and are seldom seen in the sunlight unless they are relaxing and working on their tans. Reptiles, by the way, can't roll over which is why they are always pale and untanned on the bottom. Like humans, they do not enjoy being bothered when they are relaxing and tanning. If bitten by a poisonous reptile, stay very calm (ha), wash the wound, and casually leave the outdoors to find a doctor. Do not cut and suck, do not apply a tourniquet, do not apply a cold pack, and do not lick your car battery in an attempt to electrically discharge the venom. Those things don't work and might cause significant harm. Consider carrying a product called a Sawyer

Extractor, a suction device of proven worth for field removal of some venom. Suction devices can be of great value, especially if you're alone . . . and horny.

4. LARGE MAMMALS (e.g. lions and tigers and bears, oh my!). Despite many interesting tales from the early days of the lonely mountain man concerning sexual liaisons with large mammals other than humans, encounters with wild animals, especially carnivores, should be avoided. Bears, for instance, are capable, like many sex partners, of rapid and unpredictable mood changes. Bears are, furthermore, capable of removing significant body parts which would limit future sexual liaisons of any kind. If attacked, running away, in this case, is not recommended. Humans, in relation to other species, are remarkably slow. An exception to the do-not-run rule is this: When traveling in the outdoors with someone who runs slower than you do, running away may be considered a viable option. If attacked by a black bear, say the experts, fight back. You won't win, but you may discourage the bear enough to save some of those significant body parts. If attacked by a grizzly bear, the experts continue, play dead. In most cases, you won't have to play very long because soon you'll be really sincerely dead.

Prevention of Death by Bear Attack:
1. Carry a very large gun or a small nuclear device. Neither of these will stop a bear, but both will allow you to blow your own head off before the bear tears it off.
2. Carry a can of bear repellent. This is an aerosol can of a firey substance that burns the bear's eyes and mouth. The repellent should be sprayed all over your body shortly before the bear bites you.
3. Make lots of noise while in bear country. If you've ever felt like screaming while having sex, this would be a good time to let it out.
4. While camping overnight, hang all food and other bear-attractions, e.g. toothpaste and strawberry-flavored sex oil, well off the ground. These procedures will not stop the bear from figuring out how to get the food, but peanut butter tastes better than human and, while the bear is climbing the tree, you can run away.
5. As an alternative to Number 4, leave all the food on the ground and hang your tent between two trees at least 10 feet up in the air. This technique can give a whole new meaning to the expression "swinging", but be sure you're fully awake before slipping out to freshen up. Note: In fair weather, the "Swinging Method" also works with hammocks.

6. Travel in groups of four or more. Bears mistakenly think they cannot win if they attack groups of humans, and the group, if chosen wisely, might develop into some fascinating and slightly-less dangerous liaisons.

7. Women who are having their period should sleep in the middle of the group. Men who are traveling with women who are having their period should sleep in the middle of the group. Women who are traveling with women who are having their period should sleep in the middle of the group. Everyone should have a large gun or a small nuclear device.

5. DISPELLING SEX MYTHS CONCERNING ANIMALS (e.g. unicorns, rhinos, wood nymphs). It should be noted that sexual myths surround several wild animals and, for health and safety reasons, they should be recognized as false and misleading. Unicorns, for instance, will not cure ills, including pregnancy, when they touch someone with their horns. Neither do they impart sexual virility. The horns are, however, very sharp, and may leave a nasty wound. Rhino horns are, also, reputed to be of sexual value . . . not by touching them but by eating them. Many people, even today, consider rhino horns to be a powerful aphrodisiac. First, it doesn't work. Second, you have to chew a long, long time just to get one tiny bite down. Third, rhinos have to be killed to get their horns off, and rhinos have

just as much right to life as you do. Furthermore, rhinos have just as much right to be horny as you do . . . maybe more. Note: It is not known for sure whether it was unicorns or rhinos that left humans with the expression "horny." Wood nymphs, as well as water nymphs, flower nymphs and dirt nymphs, were once thought to be the best sexual lovers on earth. It is now known that they are not, and, in fact, rhinos are slightly better.

Influential Plants

Many of the plants that grow outdoors are known for the mischievousness of the pranks they play on humans. Over the centuries sex in the outdoors has resulted in quite a bit of contact between humans and plants. This contact varies from irritating to dangerous. On the irritating end of things, plant parts are always sneaking into clothing and bedding in the outdoors and producing scratchy interruptions in an otherwise pleasurable experience. Some plants are more than just irritating. Take the stinging nettle, for instance. Stinging nettle hangs out near water, waving gently in an evening breeze, looking soft and inviting but waiting to sting and nettle. Some plants get carried away, producing effects that can be life-threatening. Even though it is assumed the plants mean no real harm, it remains in the best interest of all concerned to appreciate some of the pranks that might be played.

Poison ivy, as one example, likes to assume the appearance of an innocuous green leaf suitable for use as toilet paper. Once the oil of poison ivy (or oak or sumac) gets on skin and/or clothing, it can be passed easily from one person to another through contact. Sex in the outdoors, therefore, may result in sharing more than was expected. Learn to recognize poison ivy, and lay down somewhere else. If contact has been made, immediately wash your entire body, the entire body of your companion, all your clothes and anything else that could have contacted the plant. If someone starts to itch after washing, it means they didn't get washed soon enough, but it does not mean they still have the plant's oil on them. So it's okay to touch them. Opening Line to Remember: "Poor baby, let me scratch that for you!"

Deadly nightshade, an even more mischievous plant, grows bright red fruit all over the United States and seems to derive great mirth from pretending to be a huckleberry. People who eat the berry get a stomachache and throw up a lot. For some reason, many plants, including many domesticated vegetables, like to watch people vomit. As with all practical jokers, deadly nightshade needs to be careful. Before the berry ripens, it contains enough poison to kill an adult human. People who eat deadly nightshade get dry skin, blurred vision, hallucinations and convulsions, and a high fever. The old symptomatic saying goes like this: "Dry as a bone, blind as a bat, crazy as a loon, and hot as hell." Although that may describe some of your earlier sexual encounters, it is, generally speaking, not to be desired.

Pokeweed, sometimes called pokeberry, or just poke, is predominantly an Eastern plant that tries to trick the sexually-inclined with its name. Be warned, consumption of pokeweed has absolutely no effect on "poking." Pokeweed can be safely eaten if the leaves are boiled, the water poured off, and the leaves re-boiled. Eating undercooked pokeweed causes a burning sensation in the mouth and throat, nausea and stomach pain. Gastronomically speaking, you might as well pack in some freeze-dried lettuce.

Twenty-one species of mushrooms contain the hallucinogens psilocin and psilocybin. Hallucinogenic mushrooms have been used for thousands of years to improve sex, and were known to the Aztecs as "the flesh of the gods." Psilocybin is a relative of LSD and has some of the same effects on the human brain: mood elevation and alterations in sensation. This can be really useful if you end up with someone who isn't much fun to be with. Hallucinogenic mushrooms should be considered tricky for three reasons: 1) They are illegal in some places so you can get into real trouble. 2) They can give you a "bad trip" in which you might say and do things you regret later, which can get you into real trouble. 3) They may be mistaken for poisonous mushrooms which, when ingested, can get you into real trouble.

Climatic Concerns (Weather or Not to Do It)

1. RAIN AND SNOW. A healthy understanding of and respect for weather will do much to enhance sex in the outdoors. The first thing to beware of is clouds. Clouds are water droplets gathering together. If water droplets clump up enough for gravity to have an effect on them, they fall . . . either as rain or snow. Both rain and snow will tend to dampen your experience. Consider carrying a cagoule, the largest one you can find. Cagoules were once popular as outdoor

wear, but have, in recent years, fallen out of fashion. A cagoule is an article of clothing that is more like a small waterproof tent than a raincoat. Although there is only one head-hole in a cagoule, there is often enough room inside for two people. Cagoules also block wind. For minimum impact, choose a color that blends in with the natural surroundings.

2. LIGHTNING. The ultimate culmination of clouds and wind is, of course, a storm. In warmer months, storms may produce the greatest climatic danger to those involved in climactic pursuits — lightning. Lightning is a massive discharge of electricity directed along the path of least resistance toward the nearest object, e.g. tall things, things standing alone in open spaces. It can hurt you in several ways: 1) Direct strike, in which case the victim becomes an overdone potato chip, and sex is completely out of the question forevermore. Note: It has been suggested by sexperts that a direct strike may mimic the world's largest orgasm, but no one will ever know for sure. 2) Splash from a nearby direct strike, in which case the victim can be burned or killed. Note: Survivors of splash incidents give a variety of sensory reports none of which support the premise of the "Note" from Number 1 (see above). 3) Ground current, in which case the electrical current, running through the ground under the victim, may cause no more than a tickle, or may short the victim out totally. Note: Leg-to-leg ground current has some interesting theoretical possibilities for jump-starting people who are impotent. It worked on Frankenstein, didn't it? Stodgy research ethics committees have precluded further investigation into this area.

Close contact with lightning during sex should be avoided. It is unnecessary, if you know what you're doing, and it may be fatally dangerous. Avoidance can be achieved in several ways: 1) Stay off or leave mountains and ridges. Even moving a short distance may save your life. Lightning storms are not the time to try for a Peak Experience. 2) Stay away from bodies of water. Other bodies are okay. 3) Stay away from single trees. Married trees are okay . . . or, at least, trees that are deeply committed to each other. In fact, a forest is a relatively safe place. 4) Stay out of shallow caves and overhangs. Deep caves are okay, if they are dry, but don't touch the walls during a storm. It's actually better if you don't touch the ceiling or floor either. Try hovering. 5) Stay out of open areas where you might be the tallest thing around. Putting your partner on top does not help.

Lightning, in its dedication to reach the ground, will pass through both of you. 6) Always travel in the outdoors with someone who is taller than you are. And don't let them near you during the storm. Opening Line to Beware Of: "Oh, Sam, you give me a real tingle!"

If you are caught in a lightning storm, crouch. Crouch on your sleeping pad, if possible, to minimize conductivity. Crouching is an outdoor sexual position developed by the nomadic people of the Mongolian steppes where lightning storms are frequent. If you are in your tent when the storm hits, crouch in your tent. Opening Line to Remember: "Don't be silly, Sally, this is only for your safety!"

Variations on a Common theme: And Environmental Perspective

"Don't turn away from possible futures before you're certain you don't have anything to learn from them." Richard Bach in Illusions.

Bestiality

"My schoolmates would make love to anything that moved, but I never saw any reason to limit myself." Emo Philips.

Many people mistakenly think "bestiality" means having sex with beasts other than humans when, in truth, it means having sex like beasts other than humans. The practice of bestiality obviously dates from long, long ago when humans, relative newcomers to the animal world, watched other animals having sex in order to learn how to do it. Bestiality is limited almost entirely to mimicking mammals, with the exception of a few reptiles. Mimicking bird-sex, for instance, is almost too ridiculous to even imagine. For one thing, birds aren't physically equipped with the same general type of sex organs as humans. And, for another thing, many birds have sex while flying in the air, and it's over really really fast. Bees are even more boring and whoever came up with the term "the birds and the bees" as an expression for having sex was singularly unimaginative.

Note: It might be possible for skydivers to have sex while falling through the air if: 1) They started at a very high distance above the ground, and 2) They were very quick. It is not known if this has ever been achieved . . . or even if it has ever been attempted. It would be

greatly appreciated if anyone with knowledge concerning skydiving-sex would contact the publisher of this book with graphic details. A second volume, entitled How to Have Sex in the Outdoors: Part Two, is anticipated. Names will be excluded at the request of anyone providing information. Thank you very much.

Although it is possible for humans to have human-sex underwater (see Special Techniques), there would be no point in attempting to mimic fish-sex since they never even touch each other. Dog-sex was probably one of the first ones copied by early humans since dog's tongues hang out and it looks sort of like they're having fun. Bestiality is practiced by most humans a little bit, but it doesn't take long for humans to move on to other forms of sex since beasts other than humans are not very creative about doing "it."

Note: Historically speaking, there was a time when "bestiality" did mean having sex with beasts other than other humans. There are several reasons why the meaning changed. 1) With large mammals, and some reptiles, it proved very dangerous. 2) With the growth of the animal rights movement, it became increasingly important to show respect for wild animals. The rule of "Only Between Consenting Adults", once applied to animals other than humans, was terrifically difficult to honor, what with the language and cultural barriers. It was so hard, in other words, to know if you had the animal's consent. 3) With the increase in concern about practicing safe sex, it proved mighty difficult to know for sure if your would-be partner was carrying any disease that could be transmitted to a human. And 4) practically speaking, it was virtually impossible to establish the rapport necessary for a mutually satisfying experience.

Voyeurism
"A picture is worth a thousand words." Anonymous.

To differentiate between "bestiality" and "voyeurism", the former

means, as mentioned above, mimicking beasts other than humans having sex while the latter means just watching sex happening. Voyeurism, on one hand, may often lead to bestiality since voyeurism-in-the-outdoors is, for the most part, a trans-species form of voyeurism. On the other hand, so to speak, voyeurism may provide an addition to masturbation (see below). For people with a third hand, it can be sexual variation all its own. Furthermore, voyeurism needs to be distinguished from watching dirty movies. Watching dirty movies, and/or erotic scenes from "Wild Kingdom", does not qualify one as a voyeur because to qualify requires watching it in the flesh and/or fur.

Society, in general, looks with disgust upon voyeurism, especially as it is practiced in the city. Anyone who spends much time in the outdoors knows that it is almost impossible to not practice trans-species voyeurism, at least to some extent, and those people should not feel like a lesser person just because they stopped and stared. (Note: It is possible to be outdoors a long time and not have a chance to participate in trans-species voyeurism, say, for instance, in the northern latitudes in winter . . . unless you are a dogsledder.) If you're out for a hike or a paddle, and you happen to stumble upon a couple of wild animals attempting to reproduce their species, and it embarrasses you, you can always turn away and pretend you didn't see. But do not underestimate the stage-setting value of trans-species voyeurism. If you can afford to be a little more liberal, try pointing and saying: "Would you look at that!" Such liberalism might help set a subtle yet pervasive tone for the outdoor trip, and who knows what that could lead to. Opening Line to Remember: "Gee, Ellie, wasn't what those elephants were doing really something!"

Just in case there are no muskrats or kangaroos messing around for you to ogle as a prelude to other sexual encounters, a bit of research may still allow you the opportunity to utilize trans-species voyeurism. While the wine bottle is being passed around the campfire, you can liven up the conversation (and, maybe, redirect a few thoughts) by storing some information beforehand and dropping it casually into the chatter: "Oh, by the way, did you know that geese mate for life, but mallards, when the urge strikes them, participate in a ducky form of gang rape?" Or: "Have you heard that dragonflies have sex on the wing, the female swinging like a trapeze artist below the male?" (For more information, refer to Mark Jerome Walter's Courtship in the Animal Kingdom or, even more revealing, Robert A. Wallace's How They Do It.)

Note: A few lucky ones actually walk up in the outdoors upon two or more humans having sex. If they're real lucky, the humans having sex don't notice the voyeur, and he or she gets to watch for a while. These can be special moments and, if you're one of the real real lucky ones, you might qualify to have your story published in the Voyeur's Yearbook (see appendices for details).

Ropes and Knots

"It's been so long since I made love I can't even remember who gets tied up!" Joan Rivers.

French people, who are reportedly very skilled at sex in the outdoors, call it ligottage, but over here in America it's usually referred to as "bondage." Bondage is the art of tying up your partner before having sex, a useful skill in the really old days when unwilling partners were common and perpetuation of the species was critical. Nowadays humans have done just about all the perpetuating they need to, and bondage has become a kinky variation practiced by willing partners. (Note: The kinks are in the mind, and should not be in the rope.) The game of bondage takes a little practice so you don't screw it up, so to speak, and either waste a lot of energy you'll need later, or hurt someone.

First, it is important to work out a signal in advance in case it isn't fun anymore. Yelling and screaming, for instance, might be signs of fun or they might be signs of real distress. Hand signals don't work, of course, and code words are useless if the tied-up person is also gagged. A good signal is one that can be hummed, such as, say, the opening stanza from the Sound of Music: "The hills are alive with the sound of music." Profuse bleeding and passing out are also both pretty good signals that the fun has gone too far. Next, some rope or cord is needed, and outdoor trips usually have enough of that around somewhere. On climbing trips, seat harnesses and carabiners could be put into use. Bondage games are best played early in an expedition into the outdoors so the rope burns have a chance to heal before the return home. Triangular bandages from the first aid kit work well, and, since they're soft, they probably won't burn as much. Slip knots are the preferred knot because they can be undone quickly if you hear somebody coming down the trail or if you notice that your partner's hands and/or feet have become grossly swollen and/or blue. In extreme situations, tape or glue might work. Blindfolds should be considered if you and/or your partner are ugly.

Federal law requires that the Outdoor Bondage Safety Code be displayed prominently before the game of bondage can be legally played. A printed copy of the Code, in a waterproof cover, can be ordered from the US Department of the Interior, Washington, DC, or you can make your own. Excuse to Avoid: "I'm sorry, Egor, but you haven't posted the Code!"

Outdoor Bondage Safety Code:
1. Everyone involved must agree beforehand and sign their name and the date on the dotted line below.
2. Nothing may ever be tied around anyone's neck.
3. Nothing may ever be stuffed into anyone's mouth other than things agreed upon beforehand.
4. Nobody may ever be left alone while in bondage.
5. All knots must be quick-release.
6. Everyone involved must promise to never tell.

Group Sex
"The closest I ever came to a menage a trois was dating a schizophrenic." Rita Rudner.

When a group gets involved in sex in the outdoors, it's usually a group of men, although more and more groups of women are starting to acquire a taste for this activity (which may be one explanation for the proliferation of "women only" outdoor trips). Occasionally, in more liberated outdoor circles, both men and women are participating in group sex together. In most cases, outdoor group sex starts around a campfire, after the evening meal has been prepared and eaten, when everyone is tired but not quite ready for the sack.

A common group sex scenario often sounds like this:
First Speaker starts with, "Hey, did you see the boobs on that babe who passed us on the trail, the one wearing that little yellow halter top?"
Second Speaker replies, "Gee, did I ever! I'd sure like to take a nap on that pillow!"
Third Speaker joins in, "Nap!" Are you kidding? What I'd like to do is . . . . "

And so the evening runs on until everyone, too tuckered out to continue, goes off to their respective sleeping bags. This is not a very high-grade form of sex in the outdoors, but, being almost as old as the "deed" itself, it is undoubtedly here to stay.

On rare occasions, group sex goes beyond the verbal stage. In this case, it is especially important to maintain group safety. As the old outdoor sex adage states: The safety of the many outweighs the safety of the few. Special considerations for active group sex in the outdoors should include but are not limited to:
1. In cold environments, consider the "be like a bee" guideline. Bees, in winter, keep rotating so the warm inside bees change places regularly with the cold outside bees.
2. In hot environments, consider reversing the "be like a bee" guideline, and periodically have someone throw a pot of cold water into the center of the group.
3. In high angle environments, be sure to check the sheer and tensile strength ratings of the ropes before going hog wild. The Canadian Bureau of Outdoor Sex Standards (C-BOSS) has performed exhaustive tests and all brands of climbing rope available in North America. (Note: The Bureau is a little hard to track down. At this writing, they may be contacted at: C-BOSS, General Delivery, Whitehorse, Yukon Territory.) It is strongly advised to keep one member of the group segregated and in charge of rope management in order to prevent

entanglements that could otherwise last a lifetime.

4. On whitewater trips, special buoyancy considerations are required. As a rule of thumb, take the capacity rating of your craft and subtract two for normal group sex, and divide in half for really athletic group sex. Depending on your group, you may wish to round down to achieve an even whole number. Never round up. (Note: These rules do not apply to canoes.)

5. For in-the-ocean group sex, everyone should be required to wear a personal flotation device (PFD). It is recommended to use the buddy-body system with periodic count-off's to ensure no one has sunk in the confusion. Use of shark repellent is optional . . . but advisable.

Masturbation

"I remember the first time I had sex. It was very frightening. I was all alone." Rodney Dangerfield.

Masturbation, the skill of holding your own in the wilderness, was once considered a basic piece of knowledge, such as building a fire by rubbing sticks together, something essential to survival. But it is rapidly becoming a lost art. Nowadays, with the growing diversity of pornographic magazines and X-rated movies, the sophistication of vibrators, the availability of K-Y Jelly, and other technological advances, the old handskills are being forgotten. With the modern back-to-nature movement, and its concomitant resurgence of interest in sex in the outdoors, perhaps there will be a renewal of interest in the preservation of some of the grand old ways. Let's hope so.

Sexual Adjuncts Found in Nature

"To know when you have enough is to be immune from disgrace."
Lao Tzu.

The use of objects found in nature to help satisfy you or your partner's sexual desires is limited only by your imagination and a few rules. You're on your own with the imagination part, but here are the rules:

1. Your choice of nature's offerings should be agreed upon beforehand by all parties concerned. Believe it or not, some folks don't like the feel of salamanders.
2. Living flora are generally more accepting of a role as a sexual device than living fauna. Consider how a rabbit feels about being used in cancer research.
3. You don't have to negotiate with dead objects, but you should respect them.
4. There are soft pine cones and there are hard pine cones. There are small pine cones and there are large pine cones. Be careful!
5. Know your mushrooms well.
6. Cockleburrs, and other prickly plants, are out . . . regardless of their names.
7. Feathers are in, especially if they are no longer attached to the bird . . . unless it's a very sexy bird.

Some herbs found in nature have been used for centuries to enhance the sexual experience. If you're hiking around in Mexico or the southwestern United States, keep an eye peeled for damiana, well-known for its aphrodisiac effect. About one hour before sex, make a strong infusion of the herb by steeping 4000 damiana leaves in approximately 18 gallons of water for 10 minutes. When the water has cooled, soak in it until you're ready for intercourse. It gently stimulates the genito-urinary region. If you're in a hurry, or without an 18-gallon container, make a cup of damiana tea and drink it. It might work.

7

Outdoor Sex Etiquette

"If you can't say something nice, don't say anything at all. If you can't do something nice, don't do anything at all." Ms. Manners.

Etiquette, for those who have forgotten, means acting in a certain way because it's the nice way to act and not because you have to act that way. Law, for instance, says no one can kill Bambi unless it's deer season and a license to kill has been purchased. Etiquette, on the other hand, says no one should set their tent up in a bed of wildflowers because someone else might come along later and be disappointed by a ruined flower bed.

Minimum-Impact

Sex in the outdoors can potentially have a severe impact on an otherwise pristine wilderness area. First, consider the visual impact. Imagine the consternation of someone who comes walking over a ridge and sees the natural wonder of a magnificent vista blotted by a couple of people having sex in a high alpine meadow. Yuck! Instead, move into some bushes or into a stand of thick timber, out of the open and well away from trails. Above treeline, hiding among boulders should do. In the sandstone country of the desert Southwest, there are neat little overhangs hiding shady hidey-holes everywhere.

Lots of thrashing around in the same spot is bound to have a noticeable impact on the ground cover — crushed grass, compacted soil, etc. — and is easy to avoid. Among trees the ground is covered with duff, a dense layer of decayed matter such as leaves and pine needles, and duff is soft and comfortable and easy to restore after being thrashed around on. In the woods of the deep South, it is clearly understood that "moss be mo' bettah" . . . but watch out for the chiggers. Beaches and other sandy spots work well, too. Sometimes, even in summer, patches of snow can be found in the high country, and, if enough insulation is available, that makes a good place to use without much impact on the environment.

Sound, too, can have a negative impact in an outdoor setting. Yells and moans will carry long distances over open water and across lush, wide meadows. Those same noises will disperse quickly among trees. Boom-boxes are simply unacceptable in wilderness areas. If music is essential to your sexual experience, hum.

Natural water sources need to be protected. If you need to wash up — before or after — you can get by jumping into a lake or wading into a stream or river. Soap, however, can be fun, but it should only be used well away from water sources. Here is the way to use soap for minimum impact. Everyone takes off all their clothes and gets wet in the lake or stream and fills all the available empty containers with water. Move about 200 feet away from the water source. Everybody lathers everybody else up real good, being careful to get the hard-to-reach places, and pours the water from the containers over each other. This is usually pretty noisy so it would be best if you're in a stand of timber . . . where there's duff . . . and other people can't see you. Opening Line to Remember: "Let me scrub your back for you, Helen!"

Trash is ugly and should be collected before leaving the sex site. Check carefully for anything that could have been carelessly thrown aside in a moment of passion. Condoms can kill! A pelagic seabird washed up on the beach after becoming fatally entangled in a carelessly discarded sport-bra is a sad sight indeed! If you packed it in, pack it out. Fluff up the duff, smooth out the sand, etc. The key to minimum impact is this: Make it look as though you never came.

Campground Rules

Not everyone will want to have sex in the outdoors way out in the wilderness. If you own a Winnebago, the only rule of etiquette is keep the curtains closed, the door shut and the shock absorbers in good repair. Tent campers should keep the noise down and the tent flaps closed. The general rule is this: Be sensitive to others less fortunate than you.

And consider the little children that so often litter campgrounds. Imagine them seeing something they shouldn't see! They might grow up thinking sex was okay!

Note: In developing countries, tents are a novelty that often attract attention. I awoke in a tent in Honduras once with a mass of little brown eyes peering through the mesh door. Gee, I was glad I wasn't having sex at the time . . . sort of.

Further Note: If kids are members of the party you're traveling in the outdoors with, you probably: 1) Should plan on not having sex, and/or 2) Should bring a separate tent for the kids. If the kids are teenagers or, even worse, you agreed to chaperone a group of teenagers on a camping trip, it probably won't matter in the least that you have a separate tent. In case of teenagers, bear repellent works well . . . much better than on bears. Do not play dead. They just get more excited. Fighting back is probably the best plan.

Even Further Note: If you end up with an overpowering urge to have sex with your partner, and you happen to be sharing a tent with another couple, the time has come for some frank talk. For any number of reasons, sharing a tent with a couple who are having sex may be acceptable. Etiquette requires, however, that you bring up the matter for discussion before other things get brought up.

Safe Sex in the Outdoors

"Be a virus, see the world." Gary Larson.

Anyone having sex in the outdoors, or sex anywhere for that matter, who is not concerned about safety is either morally and ethically blind, or stupid, or both. There are three areas of safety that need to be addressed: 1) Is the environment safe? (Am I protected adequately from the cold?) 2) Is the threat of disease negligible? (Am I sure about the lifestyle of my partner?) And 3) Has the threat of pregnancy been eliminated? (Do I know how long this condom has been in the first aid kit?)

Environmental Safety
This topic has been dealt with in preceding sections of this book.

Safety from Disease
Alone at last? Maybe not! Consider for a moment, that delightful-looking partner on the other side of the tent, the one slipping into something a little more comfortable, could be infested with microscopic critters itching to take an outdoor trip of their own.

There are several ways to prevent the spread of disease through sex. One is total abstinence from sex which is, of course, totally out of the question. Another way is by taking universal precautions. To take universal precautions requires you to ask your partner: "Is there any disease in the whole universe that I could catch by having sex with you?" And your partner says: "No!" And you say: "OK, fine." Sometimes taking universal precautions does not work. (Note: Some people will say anything in order to have sex.) If one does not trust universal precautions, then one may resort to regional precautions. To apply regional precautions requires the use of a mask over the region of your mouth and nose and, if a male is involved, the use of a condom over the region where condoms are designed to go.

Note: In the event that spontaneity or poor pre-planning finds you ill-prepared, regional precautions can be improvised by using Zip-Loc bags from your backcountry kitchen kit and rubber gloves from your outdoor first aid kit. As Einstein said: "Imagination is more important than knowledge."

The greatest threat to one's well-being is undoubtedly AIDS (Accidentally-Induced Death Sentence). AIDS is a disease characterized by progressive deterioration of one's immunological system, leading irresistibly to death from all the germs of the world that can no longer be fought off by the deteriorated immunological system. It is an unpleasant way to die and, since no one would chose it as an option, it is a syndrome that has acquired the somewhat deficient name of Accidentally-Induced Death Sentence. It is a popular theory that AIDS and humans share a common ancestry, both having developed from the monkey population of Africa's wilderness. Or perhaps you prefer the theory that lets monkeys off the hook but skewers the World Health Organization (WHO) for mucking around with the smallpox vaccine. In either case, there are several ways to get AIDS, but the one of immediate concern is getting it from unsafe sex. AIDS germs are carried in human blood and in the human body fluids useful in having sex. AIDS germs are

very adaptable, and, even though they prefer the hustle and bustle of big cities (e.g., the hills of San Francisco), they may be found in the untrammeled forests of the earth's wildest land (e.g., the San Juan Mountains). The transmission of AIDS can be prevented by using any of the aforementioned methods, except universal precautions. Excuse to Accept: "We should be careful, Winona. I have AIDS!"

Hepatitis B ("B" for Bad) is another potentially-fatal disease that can be contracted while having sex. It's more common than AIDS, but, unlike AIDS, there is a very effective vaccine against hepatitis B. It takes six months for the vaccine to become completely effective, requiring safe summer frolics in the outdoors to be planned and prepared for around Christmas. Like condoms, wetsuits and tarps also provide some protection against hepatitis B and AIDS, but the sensory deprivation is astounding.

For those who are particularly fond of sex-on-the-beach, a watchful eye should be kept open for crabs. Crabs are crustaceans with four pairs of legs and one pair of pincers. It's hard to imagine that anyone could have crabs and not know it, but some varieties are small, such as hermit crabs, for instance. Give your swimsuit a close inspection before putting it back on. And watch out for those pincers!

International travel may provide an opportunity to contact some sexually transmitted disease (STD) life forms indigenous only to certain geographic locales. In Siberia, for instance, an infestation of pubic hares has been wreaking much havoc among the outdoor sexually active of that region. There is some evidence, inconclusive, that these pesty little bun-nies have been moving indoors and hiding under beds in yurts. Caution is advised. If you are anticipating overseas outdoor adventure travel, contact the Centers for Disease Control (CDC), International STD Section, in Atlanta, Georgia, for specific warnings and recommended innoculations prior to leaving this country. The CDC maintains a 24-hour phone service: 1-HOT-SEX-LINE. This same line will also provide you with treatment recommendations if you think you've already contracted an STD. Speak freely — the CDC people are very professional, although some callers report what sounds like good-natured snickering the background.

Note: You may hear a sexually active female remark about contact with an unusual life form: "That guy last night was a real worm . . . or snake . . . or slug!" Sexually active males are more often overhead talking about something fuzzier: "Man, was she a dog!" It is probably safe to assume that the critters being referred to are sexually transmitted, and, once again, caution is advised.

Of all sexually transmitted diseases (STDs), the most common and the fastest spreading is the Human Papilloma Virus (HPV). HPV is also known as genital warts, venereal warts and condyloma. There are at least 60 types of HPV, some causing genital warts and some causing warts on other parts of the body. The warts can be whitish, brownish, pinkish or flesh-colorish. They can be as large as a dime or so small they only show up under magnification. They can hurt and/or itch, but they usually produce no symptoms, which is another one of the reasons why universal precautions don't always work. The virus is highly contagious and can be spread through any kind of genital contact, not just intercourse. All you have to do is rub up against one of the warts. If a female is involved in the relationship, HPV transmission can be prevented with the use of aspirin. One aspirin is placed between the knees of the female, and held there very tightly until the urge to have sex passes. This also works for prevention of pregnancy.

Birth Control
"If God wanted sex to be fun, he wouldn't have invented children as punishment." Ed Bluestone.

There are several ways to prevent pregnancy while still having sex in the outdoors. Most of these methods work just as well indoors and are beyond the scope of this book. It should be noted, however, that camouflage condoms offer absolutely no more protection outdoors than indoors, but they are, of course, less noticeable should you accidentally leave one lying around outside the tent. The purpose of cami-condoms is to provide secrecy . . . no one can see you coming! (Note: Cami-condoms are available in Deep Forest, Desert Storm, Boulder and Duff, and all come in Lightweight and Expedition Weight.)

One way of birth control not suitable for most homes is the Cryogenic Method. Cryogenics has nothing to do with weeping, but is, instead, the science of cold and cold's effect on things. For the Cryogenic Method to work it has to be very cold outside. Just before the critical moment, all the insulation must be thrown off and the sperm freezes to death on the way out of the male partner. Timing is very important, and the Cryogenic Method of birth control has been known to fail, especially in hot-blooded partners.

Another outdoor method of birth control involves the use of herbal remedies for pregnancy. To work, these herbs must be eaten by the female relatively soon after intercourse. The most popular remedy comes from the seeds of a plant called Queen Anne's Lace. Anne, you may remember, was a famous queen who had trouble getting pregnant. Care must be taken to positively identify the plant. Plants, you may also remember, like to mischievously disguise themselves as other plants. Queen Anne's Lace is a member of the Carrot Family and, as such, looks much like the deadly Poison Hemlock, another member of the Carrot Family. An average adult female must consume approximately 200 seeds of Queen Anne's Lace to insure contraception. 200 seeds weigh about a pound-and-a-half. It is strongly advised to gather the seeds prior to intercourse. The seeds taste terrible, but may be mixed with granola. Wild yams may also be eaten to prevent pregnancy. In fact, there is a substance in wild yams that is found in many brands of birth control pills. Yams taste much better than the seeds, especially with a little butter and sugar and a bottle of a slightly-dry red dinner wine. Since they require cooking to be palatable, and cooking takes time, use of wild yams should be well-planned ahead of time. Excuse to Avoid: "Not now, William . . . the yams are still boiling!"

Note for Men Only: Remember, a vasectomy means never having to say you're sorry!

UTIs, Vaginitis and Camp Hygiene

For about 20% of all women in the United States, and as many as 5% of men, urinary tract infections (UTIs) are akin to a curse. It is more common in women because the urethra, the tube from the bladder to the outdoors, is much shorter in women than in men (or, at least, in most men). Many people who have UTIs find it difficult to discuss their problem since having sex is the most common cause. Bacteria that results in UTIs already lives on and in a person's body, and "going all the way" may move those germs all the way into the urethra. UTIs have also been associated with whirlpools, swimming pools, and carpools during long commutes, none of which are relevant to the outdoors. Typical signs of UTI include an increased need to urinate, a burning sensation on urination, and low abdominal pain. If you think you have a UTI, you should check out of the North Face Hilton and check in with your favorite doctor for some antibiotics. The best ways to prevent UTI are to 1) Stay as clean as possible, and 2) Pee often, especially after having sex. Frequent urination, which is a good idea for everyone, can be encouraged by drinking lots of wine . . . and beer, too.

Vaginitis is pretty much limited to women. Unlike UTIs, vaginitis tends to burn and itch all the time. A discharge with an unpleasant odor may be released by the vagina. Over-the-counter medications for the treatment of vaginitis are available and may be purchased ahead of time and carried in an outdoor first aid kit. Treatment also includes 1) Staying as clean as possible, and 2) Staying naked as much as possible. Opening Line to Remember: "If you want to slip out of those clothes and prevent vaginitis, Wilma, I won't mind!"

Since so much safety depends on cleanliness, a few words concerning camp hygiene are in order. Camp hygiene, in this case, refers to regular cleaning of your own personal nether regions while camping. This can be accomplished by spending a few moments each day squatting with a bucket or pot of water and a little soap. During winter and/or high altitude expeditions, snow can be substituted for soap and water. Grime simply freezes and falls off. Care must be taken to prevent other things from freezing and falling off. In addition, sexual devices should be thoroughly washed and allowed to air dry between uses.

Safe Outdoor Sex Comparison Chart

Your best bet for avoiding STDs, pregnancy, and general uncleanness while having sex in the outdoors is Know Your Partner. You can position the odds in your favor by knowing whether your potential partner falls in low-risk or high-risk group.

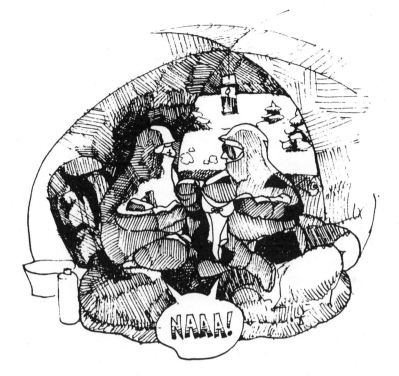

Low-Risk Group	High-Risk Group
Backpackers	Backpackers from San Francisco with Sierra Club patches on their packs
Mountain bikers	Harley Davidson bikers
Canoeists	Canoeists with "Canoeists Do It With Paddles" bumper stickers
Mountain climbers	Rock climbers, especially those wearing tiger-striped lycra
Car campers	Car campers near Grateful Dead concerts
SCUBA divers	Nude SCUBA divers and oil rig divers
Cowboys	Cowboys from the Bronx
Amateur photographers	Professional photographers
NOLS students	NOLS instructors
Outward Bound instructors	Outward Bound students
USGS surveyors	Pipeline surveyors

Low-Risk Group	High-Risk Group
Remote foreign villagers	Remote foreign villagers who live near US military bases
Church group members	Southern Baptist and Catholic Women's Church group members
Ornithologists	Archeologists
Environmentalists	Environmental lobbyists from Washington
Sheep herders	Sheep
National Park Rangers	National Park Outfitters
Large Vegetable hunters	Big Game hunters
Ginseng gatherers	Mushroom gatherers
Orchid growers	Marijuana growers
Dogsledders	Snowmobile sledders
Cross country skiers	Downhill skiers, especially the National Ski Patrol
Loggers	Loggers on Friday night
Prospectors traveling alone	Prospectors traveling with a burro
Writers	Editors

Guidelines for Sex in the Outdoors

"Touch is not only nice. It's needed. Scientific research supports the theory that stimulation by touch is absolutely necessary for our physical as well as our emotional well-being." Kathleen Keating in The Hug Therapy Book.

Creating the Mood

Ambiance is underrated. Do what you can to create a setting conducive to sex in the outdoors, a mood of quiet comfort and easy intimacy. Start the campfire early, so it has a chance to burn down to a soft, crackling glow. Use resinous woods for the fire, e.g. pine and fir. Alder and cottonwood smell bad. (Note: If you have a bad body, place the fire well-away from the tent. You don't want too much light.) Place the wine in a creek or lake to chill. (Note: In the absence of creeks and lakes, you can wrap the wine is a wet T-shirt. Evaporation will chill it admirably.) Consider decanting the wine into a water bottle before serving. Decanting allows the wine to breathe, and allows you to hide the fact that you bought a half-gallon bottle of $3.98 Red Goofy. (Note: If you bought good wine, skip decanting, and leave the pricetag visible.) Open the can of smoked oysters in time to wash off the stinky juice that invariably spills all over your hands. Make sure your last shit was well away from the tent . . . and downwind.

Preparing the Boudoir

Boudoir is technically French for a "woman's private room," but calling the tent that helps set the mood. Opening Line to Remember: "Shall we retire to the boudoir, my dear?" Unroll the sleeping pads and lay on them, checking for lumps. Remove the lumps. Unstuff the sleeping bags early, so they have time to fluff up. Shake out the pine needles from the last trip. If you brought a book of poetry, place it and a flashlight near at hand. (Note: Robert Service, perhaps, or Gary Snyder for the trendy. Haiku for the ultra-trendy.) Place a fresh roll of toilet paper near the tent door.

What He Wants Her to Know

It ain't the same for me as it is for you, but I sure wish it was! It doesn't take much to turn me on . . . almost anything will do it . . . like a glimpse of your fresh-washed underwear drying on a bush. That doesn't mean I don't respect you, or think of you, especially parts of you, as less than a person. Well, maybe it does a little bit . . . but not much! I can feel that way about your body parts and still care about you deeply. It's just that thinking about those things gets the old ball rolling. Maybe you find this hard to understand.

Part of the problem is this: You can just lie there and do it, if you have to, without much interest, but I have to have some stimulus to get the "old feller" up for the occasion. If I don't get turned on, nothing happens. I can't be "taken" or "used" like you can . . . at least not in the same way. Most of what I physically feel is in my private parts. Maybe that's why I grab for one of your private parts right away. You say you need time to get in the "mood", but grabbing parts is how I get in the mood. Maybe you could teach me how to feel with other parts.

You think I think of you as a sex object. That's true sometimes, but what I'd really like is for you to think of me, now and then, as a sex object. How about putting some of that "women's intuition" into intuiting that I'd like for you, every once in a while, to be the aggressor, to start grabbing before I do. Wouldn't that be fun? It would for me, anyway. Hey, we're way out here in the woods . . . who's gonna know?

I think the best lover would be one who stays "all woman" but jumps in about half the time like a man would. The best lover doesn't make ugly faces when I undress, doesn't attract moose with during-sex noises, doesn't fall asleep during sex, has multiple orgasms, and is well-trained in wilderness medicine.

What She Wants Him to Know

Just because it takes me longer to get going doesn't mean I don't care. If you're willing to take time, instead of wham-bam-thank-you-mam, then I know that you care, too. I get excited sometimes by being casually touched and by seeing male parts, but it seems like it takes me longer for things to build up. It appears to me as if you can get completely satisfied in a few minutes, but I can't do that. Sometimes I'm excited but you're too blind to see it, and I don't have the visible display you have to announce it. I get interested in having sex by being involved with your personality, by the unpredictable (and gentle) things you do to me, by the mood that gets created.

There are a lot of times when I don't do things to you because I'm afraid of your reaction. What would really help me is if you told me things you'd like for me to do. I don't think women's intuition is as powerful as you think it is. It seems like you expect me to read your mind. I don't mind being the aggressor sometimes, but I like being aggressed, too.

But don't be cruel! Sometimes sex in the outdoors can be pretty wild, but it should never be mean or unkind. I am a person and I am an equal. Sometimes I get really frustrated by you, by your rush and your lack of gentleness, but I think I very seldom show it.

I think the best lover is one who is sensitive to the individual woman I am. The best lover doesn't have an orgasm while undressing, always removes his boots, is comfortable in at least five different positions, doesn't get distracted by nearby bellowing moose, doesn't keep asking "How's it going?", has multiple orgasms, and gives long backrubs after sex.

Apres-Sex

Consider what you say immediately after sex. It can have a very positive and/or negative effect on the next time. Some choices of apres-sex statements include but are not limited to: 1) "Did you have the big O?" 2) "It was never like that before!" 3) "Are you hungry?"

4) "Uh-oh, the condom ripped!" 5) "Are these your socks?" 6) "Thank you very much!" 7) Where's the toilet paper?" 8) "Your T-shirt's on upside down!" 9) "I'm ready for some shuteye. How 'bout you?" 10) "Hand me the first aid kit!" 11) "Maybe you were just nervous!" 12) "Are you ready to go again?"

The Most Important Guideline
Have fun!

10

Testimonials

"Experience is a cruel and heartless teacher." Anonymous.

Good Things Come Out on Top

"J. and I reached the summit of Mexico's 5452 meter (18,000 feet) Popocatepetl on New Year's Day. Popo, a smoking volcano, is named for a famous Aztec hero who still 'carries the torch' for his dead love, Iztaccihuatl, whose name is stuck on another nearby volcano. Down below, at Tlamacas Lodge, hundreds of people were celebrating. We had climbed a route called Las Cruces and, looking back, we could see lots of climbers coming up the same route. But we had started yesterday, camped just below snow line, and topped out early. We were the only ones on the summit that morning. J. and I had been going out for a couple of months, back in Montana, and it wasn't too hard to talk her into a 'quickie', to honor the spirit of Popo, and to celebrate this special occasion. There's a summit hut on Popocatepetl, but we discarded that idea after a brief glimpse of its broken-down interior. We used the hut as a windbreak and did what we call 'sitting-sex' — I sat on my pack, and she . . . . Anyway, it totally took my breath away — literally. I'm glad we did it. It makes fond memories and a good story. But my final analysis of sex at 18,000 feet is that it's more a matter of survival than fun." B.S., Missoula, Montana.

A Rustling in the Leaves

"Here in Georgia the leaves on the oak trees turn brown and fall to carpet the forest floor every Autumn. It sure is pretty, and it smells kinda good when you pile 'em up and roll around in the pile. My boyfriend and me like to roll around in piles of leaves, and sometimes that leads to other things. My family lives on the edge of the woods, and we don't have to walk very far to find enough leaves to rake into a big pile. We were doing 'other things' one Saturday afternoon when

I heard Pa call my name. He sounded real close. I peeked up and saw he wasn't far away, but he was looking the other way. So we quietly packed a lot of leaves over us, and we lay real still. Before long Pa went back to the house. We got dressed and walked back real casual, like nothing had happened. PS. If you all try this, we recommend you bring a blanket because the leaves are scratchy." Bobby Jean, Albany, Georgia.

Beach Blanket Bingo

"Sand is always a challenge, dudes. The challenge is to keep the sand out of eyes, nose, and other moist places where it causes itching and discomfort. After years of excellent experience, I'd like to offer two pieces of advice. One, wait, if you can, for low tide and use the intertidal zone where the sand is damp and compacted. Timing is important so you don't get washed out to sea. Two, use a very large blanket, dudes. Both of these pieces of advice are virtually useless if

the wind is blowing. If the wind is blowing, use the lifeguard hut."
Hunk Harrison, Lifeguard, Palm Beach, California.

Bare Attack (Edited for publication.)

"There was just the two of us hiking in grizzly country. After dinner we had turned off the stove and we were talking quietly in the dark when the urge struck. We were going at it pretty hard, near the fire (which had died down), on an ensolite pad, with her on top, when suddenly she screamed. Screaming wasn't something she normally did, so I opened my eyes. I was just in time to witness a huge grizzly bear snatching her off me and dragging her into the woods. I have heard the smell of sex can attract a bear. Anyway, I never saw her again. I was embarrassed to tell the truth before now. Everybody thinks she just wandered off alone and never showed up again." Anonymous Person, Anonymous Town, Anonymous State.

On the Rocks

"TJ and I were visiting the Garden of the Gods near Colorado Springs when we decided to scramble up a tall stack of boulders not far from the Visitor's Center. There was one place where I had to give her a boost up a tricky spot. TJ is shorter than I am, and she couldn't reach the next ledge, but she insisted we keep going. From the top we could look down and see climbers with ropes and pitons working their way up another steeper side. This was several years ago when pitons were OK to use. It was a warm summer day, and TJ thought we could work in a little sex before the climbers reached the top. I was nervous, but that part worked fine! But we heard the noise of the climbers and realized they were almost there while we were still naked. So we hurried, with our clothes in our arms, down the side we had come up. At the tricky spot we dropped our clothes and I jumped down. But TJ, still being shorter, was afraid to make the jump. She had to lie down and slowly slide over the edge, scraping off some skin, and letting her legs down until I could reach them. This was accompanied by some very appreciative calls from the climbers. TJ loves to tell this story at parties." Bob Lickert, Pitkin, Colorado.

On the Rocks Part Two

Bob and I stopped to see the Garden of the Gods, near Colorado Springs, one summer day, and he decided we should try to climb up a very dangerous rock formation near the Visitor's Center. Other people were climbing the same rocks, sensibly using ropes to protect themselves. At one point it was so steep I told him we should turn back, but he insisted we keep climbing. He had to lift me up so I could climb over the really steep part. Once on the top, he practically tore my clothes off, telling me how exciting sex up there would be. I finally gave in when he said if I didn't he would climb down and leave me. When he was almost done, the climbers came up over the edge. We grabbed our clothes and ran for it. But at the really steep place he jumped down and left me. If I had not screamed, I am sure he would have deserted me. Finally, he came back up and helped me down. But I got some very bad abrasions on sensitive areas. The climbers seemed to think it was all great fun. I hate it when Bob tells this story at parties." TJ, Pitkin, Colorado.

Wet Dreams

"A couple of years ago some totally cool friends I had just met at school, and me, decided to run the San Juan River, the stretch from Mexican Hat on down toward Lake Powell. It was Spring Break. As the sun got hotter and hotter, we kept taking off clothes until all of us were naked and really having a totally cool time. The girl sitting next to me, I forget her name, kept rubbing up against me, and we kept getting hotter and hotter, and the beer was flowing almost as fast as the river (and some other stuff), until, I don't remember when it started, she was sitting on my lap, and we were doing the wild thing. It was totally cool, especially in the rapids. The only downer was this jerk sitting on the side of the river by a canoe who kept staring at us through binoculars." X., Logan, Utah.

Howdah Do It on an Elephant

"Please, I would not say this thing, but my good friend, Doctor Rose, has asked me to say something. So let me tell you that I am a guide in India who takes the Americans on rides on the elephant's back in very nice howdahs, I think, with cushions. There are some times when I take others who are my good friends on rides on the elephant's back when there are not the tourists to take. Sometimes we do more than only ride and let me tell you, please, that the elephant's back sways and bumps most delightfully. It is not necessary to move because you see the elephant moves for both of us. Once, I must tell you, this can be most embarrassing for the elephant when you do not guide him walks where he wishes, even into the streets of the city. Doctor Rose has also asked me to say that he has not tried this and he is my good friend also. Thank you." No name, please, Bombay, India.

Howls in the Desert

"We, George and I (maybe you should leave George's name off of this), had been hiking with a guided group in the desert country of Arizona for almost two weeks when we thought it was time to slip away, one night, to reestablish our sexual relationship. The moon was bright and it was a fairly warm night, and we were squirming around partly on the sleeping bags and partly off. Suddenly, George started howling like something straight out of hell. I jumped up and saw a scorpion rushing off. It had stung him right on the bum. He howled for about 10 minutes before he finally calmed down. I know it must have hurt, but I couldn't stop laughing. The really funny part was that several members of the group commented the next day on how active the coyotes had been that night. George recovered, but our relationship didn't." Funny Girl, Prescott, Arizona.

Rolling on the Sea

"As a physician with a private practice I have had to deal with all kinds of pathologies (sickness). This is one of my least favorite stories, but, perhaps, some of your readers may benefit from it. Before my wife and I bought our sailboat, we rented a small one out of Honolulu, and, on the first night, anchored in a semi-protected cove south of the city. Since it was our first night on board, we thought we should celebrate by having intercourse (sex) on the deck. The swells were rolling us gently but consistently, back and forth, up and down, back and forth. At first the rising and falling of the sea seemed to increase the pleasure of intercourse, but, all of a sudden, I felt an involuntary gastric emesis (puke) rising. This required an immediate withdrawal, but, unable to make the railing, I spewed all over the deck. I would, therefore, strongly recommend an acclimatization period before attempting sex-at-sea." M.D., New York, New York.

Those Dark Wet Passages

"As an instructor for a well-known outdoor school, I am often looked up to with a kind of awe by some of my students. I would never ever use my position to take advantage of a student. There was this one particular woman, however, for whom I had developed a very special feeling . . . and I could tell she felt the same about me. Frankly, I had begun to hope we could find some time alone to develop other things. As a part of a semester program, we spent a couple of weeks caving. After the introductory part of the training, she and I set out to explore a little-used system of tunnels, some of them with passages so small we could get through them only by squeezing along on our stomachs. One particularly tiny channel opened onto a beautiful little natural hall, like an underground amphitheater in miniature. While we were exploring there, simultaneously, both our carbide lamps began to fail. In the growing darkness, she began to cling tighter and tighter to me. By the time the lamps failed altogether we were pretty well clung. Although I would never ever use my position to take advantage of a student, I wasn't sure we could find our way out in the dark, and I told her that, and one thing led to another, and after a while we were going at it vigorously . . . in an attempt to comfort and encourage each other in our dire straits. Later I suddenly remembered that we could add water from our water bottles to the carbide and they would work again. So we found our way out, and everything turned out fine. PS. I would never ever use my position to take advantage of a student." Outdoor Ed, Wind Cave, Wyoming.

Mountain Biking Madness

"My friends, they call me Madman because I'll try anything once, just for the hell of it, especially on my mountain bike. Not long ago some of the guys bet me I couldn't actually have sex with my girl while actually riding my bike. Well, my girl, you could call her Madwoman because she's almost as crazy as me, she said OK. We practiced some positions, sitting on a stool in the kitchen, and picked one with me on the bike seat and her on me. There's an old dirt road through the woods not far from town, and that's where we did it. The road was bumpy and that helped. It wasn't really that good (don't tell anybody), but I won the bet. I want to tell you this, though, if you decide to try this, you should keep your eyes on the road." Room 151, Franklin Memorial Hospital, Philadelphia, Pennsylvania.

Appendix One:

Other Ways to Say "Have Sex"

"A rose, by any other name, would smell as sweet." W. Shakespeare.

Scientific Ways:
1. Intercourse
2. Copulation
3. Coitus
4. Procreation
5. Fornication

Socially-Acceptable Ways:
1. Messing around
2. Fooling around
3. Playing around
4. Going to bed
5. Sleeping together
6. Merging
7. Uniting
8. Going all the way
9. Making love

Marginally-Acceptable Ways:
1. Doing it

2. Doing the serious
3. Doing the act
4. Doing the deed
5. Poking
6. Laying
7. Getting laid

Unacceptable Ways:
1. Screwing
2. Fornication Under Carnal Knowledge
3. Humping
4. Getting a piece of ass
5. Going down
6. Getting some
7. Balling
8. Nailing
9. Playing circus

Archaic Ways:
1. Making babies
2. Knowing someone (in the Biblical sense)

Cute Ways:
1. Bumping uglies
2. Bumping fuzzies
3. Hiding the salami
4. The old in-and-out
5. Bopping
6. Doing the horizontal bop
7. The wild thing
8. Doing the laundry (small loads)

Sports Ways:
1. Scoring
2. Getting to fourth base
3. Hitting a homerun
4. Touchdown
5. Slamdunk

Military Ways:
1. Sinking the torpedo (Navy)
2. Dropping the bomb (Air Force)
3. Firing one in (Army)

Appendix Two:

Views of Outdoor Sex by World Religions

TAOISM: Sex in the outdoors happens.

CONFUCIANISM: Confucius say, "Sex in the outdoors happens."

BUDDHISM: If sex in the outdoors happens, it isn't really sex.

ZEN BUDDHISM: What is the sound of sex in the outdoors happening?

HINDUISM: This sexual experience has happened before.

ISLAMISM: If sex in the outdoors happens, it is the Will of Allah.

SOUTHERN BAPTISTISM: Sex in the outdoors happens, but not on Sunday.

METHODISTISM: If sex in the outdoors happens, feel guilty.

CATHOLICISM: If sex in the outdoors happens, feel guilty, and ask for forgiveness.

MORMONISM (For Men): Sex in the outdoors happens, with multiple partners.

MORMONISM (For Women): Sex in the outdoors happens, but not often enough.

JUDAISM: Why doesn't sex in the outdoors ever happen to us?

SHINTOISM: Sex happens everywhere, but it's best outdoors!

Appendix Three:

Rules for Outdoor Sex

"Women would rather be right than reasonable." Ogden Nash.

Decided on via consensus by the Women of America's League for the Propagation of Sex in the Outdoors (WALPSO) after very little deliberation, this codification represents the only written order of conduct for outdoor sex. Almost all the cultures of the world, however, have oral traditions, passed down from generation to generation, that say the same thing.

1. Women always make The Rules of Sex in the Outdoors.
2. Men can never ever know all The Rules.
3. The Rules are always subject to change at any time without prior notification.
4. If a Woman thinks a Man knows all The Rules, she must immediately change some or all of The Rules.
5. Women are never wrong.
6. If it seems like the Woman is wrong, it is due to a misunderstanding which was a direct result of something the Man did or said that was wrong.
7. The Man should apologize immediately for causing the misunderstanding.
8. The Woman, at any time, may change her mind about having Sex in the Outdoors.

9. The Man may never change his mind without the expressed written consent of the Woman.
10. The Woman has every right to be angry, upset and/or frustrated at any time by any sexual experience in the outdoors.
11. The Man must remain calm at all times unless the Woman wants him to be angry, upset and/or frustrated.
12. The Woman must not, under any circumstances, let the Man know whether or not she wants him to be angry, upset and/or frustrated.
13. The Man is expected to read the Woman's mind.
14. The Woman is ready for Sex in the Outdoors when she is ready.
15. The Man must be ready at all times.
16. If the Woman has Pre-Menstrual Syndrome (PMS), all The Rules are null and void.
17. Any Man who doesn't abide by The Rules can't take the heat, lacks backbone, and is a wimp.

Appendix Four:

The Chemistry of Sex

"Sex is a romantic designation for a most ordinary biological — or, shall we say, chemical? — process. A lot of nonsense is talked and written about." almost what Greta Garbo said in Ninotchka.

Thinking about sex, preparing for sex, having sex, recovering from sex, they all produce a lot of stress. And well they should, since the chemical pathways for both, inside the human body, are the same. All of that sweat, panting and flushing of the skin (the things you love!) are caused by chemicals that your body produces, chemicals that are first cousins to amphetamines (uppers): dopamine, norepinephrine and phenylethylamine. The reaction of those chemicals in your body, e.g., the euphoria, unfortunately, doesn't last very long. That's why people so often feel a let-down after having sex.

There's another chemical involved inside the bodies of people who start feeling really attached to each other. Long-lasting relationships are built on increased production of endorphins, the human body's natural painkiller, which causes soothing emotions like peace, security and tranquility. The internal production of those chemicals, sadly, will start to peter out over time, also.

One more chemical you should know about is oxytocin, the "cuddle chemical." Oxytocin, manufactured by human brains, makes mothers want to cuddle their babies, and it makes men and women want to cuddle up. It also makes orgasms better. Oxytocin production increases three to five times as one nears climax.

Why do you need to know this? Because Dr. Rose's Sex Pills contain more than twice the Recommended Daily Allowance (RDA) of phenylethylamine! and endorphins! and oxytocin! Yes, Dr. Rose's Sex Pills can rekindle the old spark and give you the lift you need to keep going. Dr. Rose's Sex Pills come in fast-release, easy-to-swallow capsules for that power punch you desire. And they dissolve quickly in wine, without leaving a traceable residue or after-taste. Dr. Rose's Sex Pills are guaranteed to work, or your money happily refunded. Use the order form enclosed with this book to order today! Ask for Dr. Rose's Sex Pills!

Warning! Use only as directed.

Note: The preceding is a paid advertisement.

Index

From Webster's New World Dictionary: index (in'deks) noun (from Latin in-dicare) to direct attention to, indicate. Formerly, a list of forbidden books or topics...other words.